Nehemiah Adams

Broadcast

Nehemiah Adams

Broadcast

ISBN/EAN: 9783744726047

Printed in Europe, USA, Canada, Australia, Japan

Cover: Foto ©Thomas Meinert / pixelio.de

More available books at www.hansebooks.com

BY

NEHEMIAH ADAMS, D. D.

BOSTON:
TICKNOR AND FIELDS.
1863.

BROADCAST.

LIGHT is sown for the righteous." It is the destiny of the good to be happy forever, with no mixed conditions, as here. Imagine fields over which you are to pass, sown with light, which springs up in countless forms of beauty, — an interminable succession of bright visions. Such is the good man's future. — "And gladness for the upright in heart."

———◆———

SUCCESS in worldly affairs is not inconsistent with eminent goodness and the approbation of God. "And David went on and grew great, and the Lord God of hosts was with him."

"THEY came to the sepulchre bringing the spices," to prepare the body of Jesus for a longer sleep. Simple, affectionate, and yet unbelieving women! He was risen. Some of our actions are of this mixed character. But those imperfect yet loving friends were kindly treated. The tomb had angels in it. These women were made the first heralds to the world of Jesus and the resurrection. Our labors may be erroneous, superserviceable, and mixed with unbelief; yet nothing is lost when done for Christ.

———◆———

"WILL be your rereward." Be not afraid of drawing back, of unexpected assaults, consequences of acts repented of, forsaken, and forgiven. The "rereward" is of special use by night. It is night with us continually, as to unseen dangers. If you press forward after God, he will not only "go before you," but be "your rereward."

MOST wonderful are the interpositions of God for his wicked people when he sees the heathen enemies proposing to destroy them. He will punish his children, but if a stranger interposes, he will take part with the children. Moreover, he will employ strangers to punish them, and then punish the persecutors. This must have vexed the heathen nations, and it must have softened the hearts of rebellious Israel. All this is for our learning. God and his people and their enemies are the same as of old.

———◆———

"THEY saw the man clothed and in his right mind, and they were afraid." The change impressed them more than the original possession. We see some who are exceedingly wrought upon by beholding a case of conversion in a relative or friend. Nothing troubles a guilty, unbelieving heart more than this.

R IDING at anchor, in some uncertainty as to the soundings and the reefs, I thought of the Bible as anchorage amidst doubts, and scepticism, and fears. Blessed book, which recalls us from wondering, vague feelings about God and futurity. It is, moreover, like an island to escaped mariners, — solid rock, and stable earth, while all around is sea and mist.

———◆———

WE would be very careful how we importuned certain men if we needed a favor of them. We would state the case clearly and fully, and leave it to their consideration, trusting to their judgment and fidelity, feeling sure of an answer in the proper time. Is there any danger, by importunity in prayer, of impropriety? Let us be clear and full in our supplication, also remembering what he "must believe" "that cometh to God."

JOHN discovered the Saviour before the rest, on the sea-shore. His quick, discerning love helped him to say to Simon Peter, "It is the Lord." Happy he who in darkness and storms can exclaim thus to his companions.

"BUT I have prayed for thee." Might we but hear this whispered in the anticipation of trial and temptation! In foresight of specially needed grace, perhaps the Advocate with the Father has made particular mention of us before God.

"WHEREFORE, let them that suffer according to the will of God,"—showing that sufferings are as really his will as obedience. To suffer well is as acceptable as to do well.

"IT was that Mary that anointed the Lord with ointment and wiped his feet with her hair, whose brother Lazarus was sick." Yes, and he died. Dear Evangelist, you seem to insinuate the tender thought that one so kind and loving to Jesus might perhaps be spared such trials. O how many such Marys there are, and with the self-same griefs. But when Christ has made one capable of loving him greatly, He is fond of exercising that love. We delight in using anything which performs its office well. So when God has an excellent case of faith, or of love, he uses it, puts it at work; and so we see why some of the very best of people have great and strange afflictions.

———◆———

GOD should be our aim and end in preaching, as well as to save souls. We should seek to save souls not merely for their sakes, but "that God in all things may be glorified."

"ACCEPTED in the beloved." One who brings an introduction to us from a very dear friend, as his friend greatly beloved, is sure of a cordial welcome. We for the time transfer our love for our friend to him, and when we come to love him for his own sake also, our love has double strength. At first he was accepted of us in our beloved. The Saviour's acknowledgment of us before God is an immediate and sure guaranty of love on the part of God.

GOD can spare any man or angel who chooses to sin. We are not essential to his glory or happiness. Past privileges, usefulness, attainments, position, are no defence, if we forsake God. "The angels that kept not their first estate he hath reserved in everlasting chains." "Having saved the people out of the land of Egypt," he "afterward destroyed them that believed not."

CONTINUED infancy in spiritual things was owing to contention, in the case of the Corinthians. So in any church, — a quarrel keeps people from spiritual growth. Few things are worse than disturbances in a Christian church. Its meetings are a refuge, and a covert, from public, domestic, private trials; but when the church is disturbed, we seem to be homeless. Woe to him who disturbs the peace of Christ's house.

———◆———

A TRULY converted man by his fall into sin may in the lapse of years be found to have been the means of vast good in keeping others steadfast. But we are inclined to think only of the scandal brought on religion in such a case. The more prompt and vindictive the detection and punishment of counterfeiting, the greater the proof that there is a sound currency, and that men value it as they ought.

MODESTY and humility should be in proportion to gifts. Gabriel is probably most meek. Moses had a greater combination of talent than any other mortal, and he was the meekest of men. Of others, take Sir Isaac Newton, Sir Joshua Reynolds, Lady Huntington, for examples.

———•———

ELISHA'S predicting to Hazael his reign and wickedness, and Hazael's fulfilment of the prediction, show that the clearest disclosures of future retribution by one from the dead would not, of themselves, deter wicked men from sin and its known consequences.

———•———

RELIGION is hostile only to that which is hostile to religion. It is no enemy to innocent pleasure, but its best friend.

WHAT mysteriousness is there in moral culture, development? None at all. Yet this with many is conversion. But Christ represents regeneration as a mystery, and likens it to the mystery of the wind. Now what have I ever experienced, what do I preach, as to Regeneration, which makes me feel the appropriateness of the Saviour's illustration, "so is every one that is born of the Spirit"? —He experiences something more mysterious than merely changing his views. That does not satisfy the illustration of Christ.

———◆———

"CHIEFLY that unto them were committed the oracles of God." This reason assigned for the pre-eminent advantage of the Jew over all others, namely, that he received those communications from God of which the Old Testament is a record, is a powerful confutation of modern cavils against the elder Scripture.

"OBTAINED promises." This cannot mean, obtained their fulfilment; — but they who are here spoken of, by their faith in God led Him to make promises to them. He was pleased with their spirit and behavior, and in consequence promised them surprising blessings. Witness Abraham, Jacob, David, Solomon, Hannah, and others.

———◆———

THE sight of a great procession, or crowd, stirs up feelings of love, at times, in every good mind. Each of this multitude is as precious to God as I. Each has a history, a present experience, a destiny; God knows each, — his name, abode, calling, his character. Each had a parentage, an infancy, a home; there are those to whom he is dear. It is good to look on great companies of our fellow-men. It makes us humble, benevolent; it makes us feel our need of the particular love and care of God.

1*

IF heaven were apparent, desires for it might be less pure. Its external glory and beauty, its rest, its society, its pleasures, might abate our pursuit of holiness, which we now feel is the chief characteristic of the place. It would also, perhaps, too much abate the fear of death, which now has a controlling influence upon us. "We walk by faith, not by sight."

———

"THOU sowest not that body that shall be." Strange that one who has seen an ear of corn with its wrappings, its silk, its rows of kernels on the large, hard cob, all from one grain, which "cannot bear fruit except it die," can be an unbeliever in the resurrection. Moreover, such things in nature should make us exult in the thought of future bodies immeasurably in advance of the present. "It doth not yet appear what we shall be." But "we shall be like Him."

IT is greatly helpful, and encouraging too, to read God's remonstrances and upbraidings at Israel's departures from Him, his earnest wishes that they had continued faithful, and his promises if they will return,—all designed to show us what it is which God desires in us, these things being recorded not as mere chronicles, but to instruct the world by illustration rather than by a code of dry, abstract rules.

———•———

"THOU wilt make all his bed in his sickness." Some expressions of condescension on the part of God, like some acts of the same kind on the part of the Saviour, are beyond our conception. But let us not be faithless, but believing. We must not take our own measures with us in judging of God. His ways are not as our ways in showing kindness, nor his thoughts as our thoughts. If they had been in times past, how poorly had we fared.

THERE was a seeming inconsistency between Noah's preaching and the size of his ark. Suppose that multitudes had been converted? Hence, did not God intend that they should not repent? Answer: So men cavil about God's purposes and his invitations. If multitudes had believed Noah, they too could have built arks. Perhaps they would have prevented the flood.

———♦———

"SLEEP in Jesus." Beautiful words. They are not said to sleep in their winding-sheet, in their shroud, in their coffin, in their grave, but, first of all, they "sleep in Jesus," and in the same sense they continue "asleep" in him, while they live with him in heaven;—for one characteristic of the Bible is that it describes things as they appear. The identification of believers with Christ is brought to view in this Christian synonyme for death,—"sleep in Jesus."

I CAN see no sufficient reason in myself why I should be forgiven, says a sinner. True, and therefore God says, "I, even I, am he that blotteth out thy transgressions for mine own sake." Are you not willing to be forgiven, if God may get honor by it? Plead that as the reason why you may look for pardon and salvation.

———◆———

THE condescending kindness of God, and his care for his Church, are illustrated in his first revealing his name, Jehovah, in connection with the deliverance of Israel out of Egypt.

———◆———

NO one can long be a secret follower of Christ. "He entered into an house, and would have no man know it; but he could not be hid." If Christ be in you, it will be known.

THE fearlessness with which the Bible asserts divine sovereignty, decrees, divine agency, irrespective of cavils and philosophical objections, should at least keep us from dwelling wholly on the side of human accountability. "For God hath put in their hearts to fulfil his will." The two things are equally true, and they coexist.

———◆———

WE may fear for the piety of one who believes in Christian perfection in this life. There are two reasons: he has probably never seen the plague of his own heart; and he does not seem to trust wholly to the righteousness of Christ. A man who feels that he can be sinless, does not know the spirituality of God's law; and thinking so much of his sinlessness, he does not, like Paul, have that self-renunciation which they have who are "found in him, not having their own righteousness."

"FORBEAR thee from meddling with God." This was good advice, though from a heathen king, and it must have been a great reproof to Josiah. We must learn when to yield before the force of circumstances, and change our plan; and when to refrain from interposing, however kind our intentions may be, in the affairs of others.

———◆———

WHEN we speak against acting with a view to reward, we are in danger of being wiser than God. We may trust him with the morality of the motives which he proposes. "Be not overmuch righteous; why shouldest thou destroy thyself?" There is no danger in doing anything and everything with a view to the Divine approbation. Think of Moses: "For he had respect unto the recompense of the reward." Think of Christ, "who, for the joy set before him, endured the cross."

"YE are as graves." Graves are sometimes covered with Italian marble, beautiful images repose upon them, green sods, flowers, adorn them, the small bird builds her nest in the grass; the eye is charmed, the heart touched; we linger there. Then there are graves where there are but slight signs of interment, the mounds, if any, are sunken, and men walk over them. In both, a disclosure would fill us with horror. Ye are as graves! What an image have we here from Him who spake as never man spake.

THE Few. — There is "a few" in every church who are the heart. — The few save the many. — The few do most of the work. — Christ began with a few. "Many are called, but few are chosen." Some formerly proposed to render this, "choice ones." The truth would warrant this translation better than the Greek.

ON pleasing God. — If we live a good life, we shall always be likely to do some special act which will greatly please God. Abraham's offering of Isaac was not a solitary act, but the result of a good state of heart. But it secured for him the promises. God will furnish us with opportunities for special acts of obedience, if we live near to Him.

———◆———

OUR nature, it seems, is capable of a personal union with Deity. Strange that this truth as set forth in the person of Christ should meet with opposition. It opens to us an inconceivable prospect as to the capacities of the soul. Can Deity personally coexist with our nature, act through it, retain it forever, — not assuming it for a temporary purpose, and then laying it aside, but through eternity using it as a medium of manifestation? "It doth not yet appear what we shall be." "But — we shall be like Him."

THERE is an important difference between love and kindness. Some love you who really are not kind. Again, we may be kind where we may not love. The two things go well together; and loving-kindness is most beautiful. God uses the word often in speaking to us.

———◆———

PAUL makes asseverations that he did not "lie" in what he said. Were his friends so untruthful when pagans that they now needed strong assertions? There are cases in which we must not stand upon our dignity, but deny, assert, assure, and use protestations of truth and innocency.

———◆———

O THAT this could be said of us: "And by their prayer for you which long after you for the exceeding grace of God in you."

THE power of present discouragement to make us forego all our previous hopes and expectations, and to practically annihilate the promises of God, is illustrated in Elijah, who seems to have had some intimation of his future translation to heaven, but under. the juniper-tree offers to relinquish that distinction and privilege, saying, "Take away my life, for I am not better than my fathers"; so let me die as they died, only be it now. — God was better to him than he and we would be to ourselves, could we have our desires.

———◆———

ONE frequent cure of religious despondency, when it is not owing to bodily distemper, is, a clear apprehension of the distinction between Faith and Hope. We are not justified by Hope. That is not the ground of pardon. Remember him " who against hope believed." There may be faith where hope seems to be out of the question.

IF one will reflect upon the nature and number of his religious opportunities, his instructions, his liberty to be alone for reflection, his calls from the pulpit, from providence, and in his conscience, his Sabbaths, his years of Christian privileges, he cannot but see that he might have saved his soul a thousand times, and that there is no reason why eternal consequences should not follow even this short life.

"WE pray you in Christ's stead." A high commission. And how would Christ "pray you"? "Lord, teach us to pray," in this sense also.

THEY who fear God need not be afraid of him; but they will be sure to be afraid of him who do not fear him.

WE all seem to take it for granted that few comparatively will be lost. Some say it to apologize for future punishment. But the majority may be lost, and illustrate to other beings what sin can do, seeing that only a minority of those for whom God became incarnate accepted his redemption. By all calculations, so many will perish as to make endless punishment as great a mystery as though there were a thousand times more. This world is not the universe.

———

THERE is great power in a friendly visit, a single call, at the right time, under certain circumstances, and with benevolent motives. Gifts and alms are well, but your presence is the greatest attention. A call well devised and properly made sometimes has influence for life. "When he was in Rome, he sought me out very diligently and found me. The Lord grant unto him that he may find mercy of the Lord in that day."

NO subsequent good conduct can restore men to Christian society if they do certain evil things. He who yields to certain temptations must know that it is for his life. The rigor of public moral sentiment in this direction is a safeguard to virtue.

———•———

THE design of Christ's death is to save the elect, while it is sufficient for all. The clear and full belief of this will exalt our conceptions of his love to the Church, that is, to the individuals composing it. "Christ also loved the Church, and gave himself for it."

———•———

IF God uses others, and not us, to glorify him in undesirable ways, we ought to be grateful, and more zealous, and more useful, and watch.

SOMETIMES you question whether everything is not an illusion, even the great verities of the Christian faith. It is a vaporish state of mind. Do not give utterance to it except in prayer. Look into the Bible, turn over the pages here and there, and something will strike you with the force of reality. Some feelings cannot be reasoned down, for they did not come through reasoning.

———◆———

BEGIN with Love. Anything which makes you love will make you penitent and believing. Instead of trying to excite grief for sin, and faith, fix your grateful love on the Saviour, and everything else will flow in upon your heart. "Her sins, which are many, are forgiven, for she loved much." She loved before she was aware that she had saving faith, or true repentance. Love involves them. Love is not only the fulfilling of the Law, it is the fulfilling of the Gospel.

"GOD was manifest in the flesh." Fearlessly spoken. Let us dwell upon it more, in its literal acceptation. The Supreme Deity of Jesus Christ is the corner-stone of Christianity. It is infinitely grand, ennobling. It shapes our whole belief. All our views of God depend upon this. The union of God in Christ, — the God-man, — is the all-important truth.

ASSURANCE of faith, and joy, are not the chief evidences of acceptance with God, as we incline to make them. Self-loathing, and humility, are as good signs of grace as they.

JEHOSHAPHAT'S weakness was, alliance with bad characters. How foolishly he went into it, in the case of Ahab, and of Ahaziah, 2 Chron. xviii. and xx.

TO leave men free, yet accountable, is infinite wisdom. God does not govern men as he governs planets. To govern them while they are at the same time wholly responsible, is the great mystery and the divine glory of his administration.

WE carry our disposition, temper, and manners even into our treatment of our God. How do we behave ourselves toward him? Are we agreeable companions for those heavenly visitors who say, "We will come unto him and make our abode with him"?

IN vain do I urge against God's mercy,— I am a sinner. That is provided for. "When we were yet without strength,— Christ died for the ungodly."

IT is a great and good thing for God to give us a heart for any duty or event. With the heart in it, a labor, or sacrifice, or an event, becomes changed. Difficulties disappear, the complexion of things is altered. We become qualified at once for a difficult situation to which we are called, by having another heart given us. King Saul was thus favored. He shrunk from promotion. God gave him another heart, a spirit and frame of mind congenial with his new duties. It was not "a new heart," but it was good, and it was an unspeakable help.

THE sublimest truths are familiarly employed in the Bible for personal application. "Let this mind be in you which was also in Christ Jesus, who, being in the form of God, thought it not robbery to be equal with God," &c. — Notice the exhortations to "servants," leading directly to the grandest propositions concerning the Christian system.

TWO things are essential if a man would preach any considerable time to the same people, viz. "Long-suffering and Doctrine." Without long-suffering, he will be wearied by want of success and by his various trials; and without doctrine he will be vapid, a mere exhorter, draw from an empty well, drive away the thinking portion of his hearers, or make them turn him away for one who will feed them with knowledge as well as emotion. Paul, the preacher, knew what he did when he was led to use those words, "long-suffering and doctrine."

"EXERCISE thyself unto godliness." The word in the original refers to Gymnastics. Practise in being good. Use means, arts, self-denial, labor, be ingenious in seeking to be godly. It is not a matter of course to be godly. It requires practice, training, exercise. The exhortation was to Timothy, a minister, from the great Apostle.

CHRISTIANS should make a study of Christian morals, and seek to be exemplary in morality. The world appreciates that, and cannot understand spirituality. But if men see Christians made better in that which is the world's religion, that is, morality, it leads them to think that there is a reality in Christian experience.

———◆———

"I KNOW how well my heart hath earned
    A chastisement like this,
In trifling many a grace away
    In self-complacent bliss."

Great penetration and self-knowledge are in these words. There is a spiritual luxury, and spiritual pride. Work is one antidote and cure. Some Christians are like sponges on the rocks at Corfu, now dry, now filled with water, then dry, to be saturated again. And there they cleave and cling to one spot, and do no good. The ocean of divine truth only fills them, while they ought to be emptying their gains on others.

THERE is misanthropy sometimes among those who profess to love God and their brother also. They avoid intercourse and contact with others. The cure is, to mix with others in order to give pleasure, not to get it; "not to be ministered unto, but to minister." To shun society, and shut one's self up in himself, is less than human. "Then the beasts go into dens, and remain in their places." It is the cold which makes them do so.

———•———

TAKE example from Christ, sitting on the well, and talking with one person, no matter whom. How she spread his words. And what words they were! The doctrine of the universality of acceptable worship was propounded there, and the axe laid at the root of prescription and formalism in religion. We must not be penurious of our thoughts, nor refuse to preach our best sermons on rainy days to a few hearers.

"THERE is that for bashfulness promiseth his friend, and maketh him his enemy for nothing." (Ecclesiasticus xx.) A too ready way of assenting and agreeing with another, from fear of saying No, and then finding that the engagement is impracticable, and thence an affront given by seeming indifference or want of faithfulness, are referred to in this wise observation of human conduct. Lasting alienations have grown up in this way, and all "for nothing."

NEVER make a mistake, meet with a disappointment, suffer, lose anything which you prized, or go through any sorrow, without causing it to be a source of instruction. "Who, passing through the valley of Baca, make it a well." True wisdom this, instead of abandoning ourselves to grief. Rather say, What am I to learn, be, do, as the result of this trial? So dig in the valley of sorrow; it is full of springs not far below the surface.

IT must be a great satisfaction to a good man, after the day of judgment, to feel that he has had his heart and his life ransacked, turned inside out, everything explained, defined, acknowledged, confessed, forgiven, settled ; and thenceforth no more need, with him, of judgment days.

SOME people suffer long and bitterly, and do not concern themselves to know the cause. "Then there was a famine — three years, — and David inquired of the Lord," and he said, "It is for Saul and for his bloody house, because he slew the Gibeonites."

"WHERE also our Lord was crucified." Earth seen from other worlds is perhaps designated by this event, irrespective of latitude and longitude upon its surface.

DIFFICULTIES with the truth are in danger of making us part company with Christ. "This is an hard saying, who can hear it? — From that time many of his disciples went back and walked no more with him. Then said Jesus unto the twelve, Will ye also go away?" So a personal attachment to the Saviour helps us to understand, or at least to receive with meekness, many difficult things in religion.

———♦———

WHAT a glorious creation Christ is, as God-man. "He is the beginning (stands at the head) of the creation of God." So he is the goal for which our nature is to run.

———♦———

IF one can bring himself to admit the Godhead of Jesus Christ, it will prove a solvent for a great many difficulties in religion.

TALKING plainly, patiently, and to your utmost satisfaction, with argument and illustration, to one who differs from you, but is willing to hear, you are perhaps surprised to find how little impression you have made upon him. So one who had tried to give a blind man an idea of the distinction between colors was affected when the poor man quietly remarked at the close, "I have an idea that red is something like the sound of a trumpet." "The natural man receiveth not the things of the Spirit of God." "Nicodemus answered and said unto him, How can these things be?"

———◆———

THE Psalms of David are true theology. Poetry, in its true sense, is the highest effort of the human soul. Religion expressed in the Psalms is the vital action of the renewed heart. The distinction is a very nice and critical one between the theology of the intellect and the theology of the feelings.

"LEST if thou be silent unto me, I become like them that go down into the pit." How indispensable communion with God had become to this man! It should be painful, nay, distressing to us, not to have God make us feel that he regards and hears us.

IT would be good to live through a week with the Sabbath in anticipation. It would be likely to be a good Sabbath to us. It would shed its light forward into the next week, and meet the coming Lord's day.

APPLY those sublime words to perished hopes, lost fortunes, departed joys, clouded prospects, ill success, — "I am the Resurrection and the Life." They are as true of these as they are of our dead bodies.

"PREPARE a place for you." — Then everything is not already fixed and settled, with monotonous uniformity, like the twenty or thirty tenements in a block of buildings. But there will be adaptedness to our tastes, our characters, our conduct, our connections, our future occupation. "I — prepare a place for you," I, who, as man, know and appreciate all your feelings and wishes. His eye is on us while he is preparing our place. He may be influenced in his preparation by his observation of us.

> "He lives, my mansion to prepare;
> He lives to bring me safely there."

―――♦―――

WE have never had a true conception of grandeur, we shall say, when we see the second coming of Christ. "He shall come in his own glory, and in the glory of the Father, and of the holy angels." Distinguish between these, and then combine them.

WHAT "change" did Job refer to? "If a man die, shall he live again? All the days of my appointed time will I wait till my change come." Was not resurrection in his thoughts? He had been speaking of living again. Moreover, see the next verse: " Thou shalt call, and I will answer thee; thou wilt have a desire to the work of thy hands." A believer in the Resurrection feels that there is something in these words which a cold-hearted, sceptical neologist will prove, perhaps to demonstration, can by no possibility be derived from it.

THAT festoon made by the Aurora Borealis, August 28, 1859, seemed to be directly over your dwelling. A million of people probably thought the same, each of his dwelling. So the Bible is all yours, all its promises, its God, its Saviour, all yours, as though there were not millions to share them with you, and think the same.

BECAUSE "Billingsgate" became what it is, say only one hundred and fifty years ago, therefore there was no vituperative language previous to that time! Such is the argument, translated, of those who say that, because Gehenna became such as it was about such a year, therefore there was no hell previously. Moreover, inasmuch as Jerusalem rose only with the kings of Israel, there was no heaven before, because a familiar name of heaven is "Jerusalem."

REWARDS from God are mercy. "Also unto thee, O Lord, belongeth mercy; for thou renderest to every man according to his works." We should call this justice. Not so to a sinner who has forfeited everything. It is infinite mercy to reward the works of one who can do nothing meritorious in the way of justification. This is an indirect assertion, in the Old Testament, of the great idea of salvation by grace.

DAVID with some seems to be less confident in hope after his fall than before, judging from his Psalms. See the ineffaceable influence upon the soul, of transgression!

THEOLOGY is not mere knowing for the sake of knowing; but to live nearer to God. A theologian ought to have fervent piety, unction. Otherwise, he is mere lead-pipe or water-log.

THERE are exquisite touches of beautiful social feelings in Paul's Epistles. Here is one: "For he longed after you all, and was full of heaviness, because that ye had heard that he had been sick." It is a refinement of love, indeed, to yearn after those who had had solicitude for our affliction. Such refinement the religion of Jesus produces in pagan bosoms.

WE do well to conceive, if we can, what a change of affairs there will be when this whole mediatorial kingdom comes to an end. The principles of it now run through all our social existence, enter into all the dealings of God with us, both in his common providence and in his grace. To withdraw this mediatorial element is like withdrawing caloric or oxygen from nature. "Who shall live when God doeth this?" "Then cometh the end, when He shall deliver up the kingdom to God, even the Father."

———◆———

JOB tells us (ch. xxx.) how, as a magistrate, he had dealt with the wretched scum of society, the pestilent fellows, the plunderers, the villains of his day. But now, he says, in his adversity, they return upon him. His description of them, and of the indignities which he suffered from them, is a vivid picture of future misery in the next world from a similar source. "Gather not my soul with sinners."

THE pleasures of sin are very sweet; let us not deny it. But "the pleasures of sin for a season,"—this expression warns us of the bitter end. The everlasting loss of pleasure will be aggravated by the recollections of it. Suppose the desires of sinners to be eternal. Dante pictures this like no one else. Some dear young friends, with everything to tempt them, wisely say, We wish to be happy forever, and our bliss will begin when that of the devotee of the world ends. Besides, we are happier now than he.

DOES Job now curse the day of his birth? Far different would his language be could he now return and suffer. The book of which he was the occasion is worth to him a thousand times all his tribulation. When we are plunged into great and strange trials, let us look forward a thousand years; let us imagine what fruit God may be purposing to raise out of our affliction.

THE silent influence of a pious home is illustrated by the Prodigal Son. Had that home been repulsive to him, or had his father been a stern, forbidding man, that recovering thought about home would not have visited him. Take courage, parents of prodigals, if you were faithful with God and your family altars. Persevere, parents, in family religion. It may be like the fabulous song of the sea in the shell, to the ear of a child when far from home and from God.

CONSIDERING the Incarnation, the Sacrifice, the Resurrection, Ascension, Mediatorship of our Lord, not to obey from the heart his commands in the Gospel, is justly declared a crime, subjecting us to the wrath of God. Substitute an earthly parent, husband, master, for Christ, and suppose all to be done which Christ has done, and how would we regard a corresponding neglect and disobedience?

NATIONS losing the knowledge of the true God, have not at once had it restored to them. They who dwell exclusively on the paternal character of God cannot explain this. Were the relation of father the only type of God's relation to man, he would have hastened to restore his worship to the descendants of those who once knew but forsook him. "Who in times past suffered all nations to walk in their own ways." And how did they walk! See here the retributive and vindictive element in the Divine administration.

COUNT up special instances of Divine interposition in your history, cases in which God signally appeared for your relief. How many do you find yourself able to recall? Then read, — "And the Lord was angry with Solomon because his heart was turned from the Lord God of Israel, which had appeared unto him twice."

"MINE hand shall not be upon thee." Conscious of receiving a great wrong, it has wonderful power to forbear retaliation. We are thereby made superior to the evil-doer. We leave the case with God. Soon the thought of God as an avenger makes us pity, and even love, the adversary.

"HUMBLE yourselves, therefore." You have met with a great blow. The first thing to be done is to bow down before God. Wait for no explanation, consolation. Your place is in the dust at once.

THERE are four different ways by which men expect and propose to be saved. One is Fate. Another is Chance. A third is Self. The fourth is Christ.

REPENTANCE and faith may be included in some one act when the soul is unconscious of repenting or believing. The publican in the temple probably was not aware that he was complying with the terms of salvation. The woman that was a sinner probably made no analysis of her feelings when she wept at the feet of Christ. Her love was repentance, faith, submission, consecration, all together.

IT brings tears to think how kind God is to reward our poor efforts for him, representing himself as laid under obligation. "God is not unrighteous to forget your work and labor of love." The intimation seems to be that God would esteem it "unrighteous" in him not to reward us,—instead of reminding us that we are unprofitable servants, and that we never do more than our duty. What a God we serve!

"CALL the poor, the maimed, &c. Doing good to such serves to prevent wrong motives in charitable acts, and excites a pure, disinterested love, which is most like the love of ministering angels, who get no reward from us. It is also kindred with the love of God toward us and the pure compassion of Christ.

"AND Judas also knew the place." There is a history in that line which the mind of John might portray with divine pathos. That place is portrayed in the thoughts of Judas, in "his own place." He went there from Gethsemane. Shall we?

ONE is interceding for us in heaven:— "Sit ye here while I go and pray yonder." Let us watch with him.

WHILE we must give no directions to a sinner which he might be using and yet perish, there are undoubtedly means of conversion which are profitably employed. Put yourself in the way of the Holy Spirit. Go where you think he is. Avoid things which you know hinder conversion. "And ye shall seek me, and find me, when ye shall search for me with all your heart."

―――♦―――

NO doubt some lost sinners will be exasperated when they see how God spares their companions in guilt, and saves them though as deserving of perdition as themselves. What partiality! they might say. No doubt they resolve that such a being is not fit to reign. Perhaps they declare that they would rather suffer, than love and serve him. But there were instances in which others were cut off, and these complainers were left.

"YET all this availeth me nothing so long as I see Mordecai the Jew sitting at the king's gate." The folly of cherishing animosity against a fellow-creature, brooding over your prejudice, conversing about it. Rather go and see him, and find something in him, as you will, to qualify your feelings. Shall one worm of the dust make you wretched? spoil every pleasure? cover even the face of God?

———

TO see beauty is to love it. Hence all who do not love God do not know him. No matter whether prejudice, or antipathy, or consciousness of sin, be the cause, the man who does not love God does not know him. All such are "Gentiles that know not God." Yet all beauty dwells in him as its source. The conception of every beautiful thing was with him. Not to love God, then, is entire depravity.

"BEFORE Abraham was, I am." "Then the Jews took up stones again to stone him." The human heart has strong repugnance to the superhuman nature of Christ. It requires the submission of our reason to faith. It is such an infinite privilege to have such a Saviour and friend as Christ, the God-man, must be, the wonder is that all are not prejudiced in favor of his deity.

———♦———

WE do not feel at liberty to praise a distinguished man to his face. But we can tell God all our feelings toward him, and offer praises to him continually. "O thou that inhabitest the praises of Israel."

———♦———

SUPPOSE that Christ interceded as we pray. How can we expect him to do better than we? If the client is not in earnest, can he blame his advocate?

"MORE than twelve legions of angels." We should have them at our side, "presently," if we needed them. Perhaps we have them now. "And behold the mountain was full of horses and chariots of fire round about Elisha."

DANIEL showed his wisdom in simply doing "as he did aforetime," when the decree was signed forbidding prayer except to the king. He did not increase his seasons of devotion, so defying the law; he did not lift up holy hands with wrath.

"AND Jonah rose up to flee from the presence of the Lord." It is easy to do so without going to Tarshish. Avoid prayer. Live in a known sin. Neglect known duty. Be worldly-minded. Desecrate the Sabbath.

WHEN we have prayed for direction, God leaves us in perplexity, exhausting our strength, till at last we hit upon a plan, seemingly by accident. God thus hides himself, while really at work for us, to conceal his agency, and exalt the duty of effort, and to preserve and honor human responsibility.

———•———

THERE are very many instances in the Bible, plainly right, in which our instincts would surely have been at fault. For example, Christ's washing his disciples' feet; giving them that repast on the sea-shore, — the fire being kindled by him, and the fish laid thereon; sitting on the ass in his entrance to Jerusalem; several directions of a personal nature to the prophets; Moses shut out of Canaan, &c., &c. Our moral sentiments, then, are not the standard for God's administration. We must correct our moral sentiments, as we do our chronometers, by a standard.

CHRIST, apprehended by the affections, and making himself an inmate of the soul, shortens distances, lightens labor, turns despondency to cheerfulness, relieves us of burdensome responsibility, making us feel that he is working in us, by us, and for us. "Then they willingly received him into the ship, and immediately the ship was at the land whither they went."

———◆———

IN the stillness of Sabbath mornings, the prevailing frame of mind, thought, subject on which we dwell, is apt to show what our prevailing frame has been during the week. It rises to the top.

———◆———

THERE is a remarkable frequency, in the Bible, of the expression "love mercy," as applied to man.

THINK of the law of God being entirely satisfied, for Christ's sake, with a good man, in his life and conversation, who truly believes in the justifying righteousness of Christ. "That the righteousness of the law might be fulfilled in us, who walk not after the flesh, but after the Spirit."

———◆———

THE soul will forever have its deliberate choice, formed here, and persisted in. "The fruit of his doings," "the reward of his hands," will characterize every man's future condition.

———◆———

"AND the prisoners heard them." Christian joy sometimes has a deep effect on a sinner, by the contrast between his sad and wicked heart and a singing, light-hearted Christian.

"I ENTERED into thine house; thou gavest me no water for my feet." When may Christ be said to have been in our dwellings? How was it at the time of those special blessings, happy returns, great sorrows and joys? And how did we treat him? Was it thus? "My head with oil thou didst not anoint." "Thou gavest me no kiss." It seems that the Saviour looks for tokens of our love, appreciates them, misses them.

ARE we in danger of forgetting the Father, in the work of redemption, in our gratitude and love to the suffering Saviour? Read the "ascriptions" at the end of Dr. Watts's Book III. of Hymns. They instruct us on this point. "Giving thanks unto the Father, which hath made us meet to be partakers of the inheritance with the saints in light." "Giving thanks unto God and the Father by him."

THAT cannot be healthful piety where there is no activity in doing good. There is danger of luxuriously enjoying religious ordinances. We are in danger of spiritual sloth. Solomon seems to have great antipathy to sluggards, and we need to apply his words chiefly to spiritual things. He is wise who mixes reflective and meditative piety with efforts to do good and to communicate.

"BLESSED are they that keep judgment, and he that doeth righteousness at all times." (Ps. cvi. 3.) For the first and only delinquency may be fatal. Departing once from a good rule has often led to a fire, or bankruptcy, or an accident. It is not safe to do wrong in a single instance. The critical moment, the test, may now be upon us. How little you thought that that one act, so contrary to your habit, would come to light, and give a wrong and an injurious impression.

SOME things in the manner of the New-Testament writers, in speaking of the coming of Christ and the end of the world, greatly resemble the prophetic way of the old seers. Prophecy was ceasing, but those things are lingering streaks of it in the sky.

THERE is calmness in Divine justice. How slow; how long it waits; how many different things it suffers to mature for one purpose; how quietly it inflicts its sentence. "Fury is not in me."

WHEN Christ says, "He that is not against us is on our part," it is a reflection on human nature, — as though it were generally against him, and if not so, it is an exception.

SEE the great billows assailing the "small ship" with Jesus in it. Would that the disciples had had faith to rebuke the winds and seas without awaking him. Would that we could always do that which it seems so desirable for them to have done.

"IF any man's work shall be burned, he shall suffer loss." And a great loss it will be, to behold one's life a failure. Perhaps a minister here and there may find that, by some great misconception of the truth, he did no good, though he himself is saved; yet so as by fire.

HOW we anticipate an engagement with an important personage. We prepare ourselves. — We are soon to meet God "Prepare to meet thy God."

CONSCIENCE is capable of being educated, and greatly needs it. Sometimes it is morbid, needlessly sensitive, leads us to be over righteous, painfully and uselessly scrupulous. Our instincts are not the supreme law. The word of God is the rule. "A good conscience," in the wide sense of that term, is an inestimable blessing. Good sense is inseparable from it. It is in itself common sense.

———◆———

DISTINGUISH between David's consciousness of rectitude (Ps. xviii.) and spiritual pride, or self-righteousness. We honor a suitable self-esteem, and we despise that derogatory way which some have in speaking of themselves. While we must not think too highly of ourselves, and are commanded "to think soberly," there is a way in which "we ought to think." Self-respect is essential to comfort, and without it we forfeit esteem.

THERE is power in candidly stating an objection to our side of the question, without undue anxiety to answer it. "But the Pharisees said, He casteth out devils through Beelzebub, the chief of the devils." No reply. The allegation is left to candor. There is moral sublimity in this.

———◆———

WE must "labor to enter into that rest." We are not going thither as a matter of course. The means of being saved are as much decreed as our salvation. If we use no means, we may not expect the desired end.

———◆———

DEATH should not seem to us like the breaking down of a carriage in an unfinished journey, but the orderly end of a plan. "I have finished my course," says Paul.

No part of sacred history better illustrates the subject of Divine decrees and free agency, than the history of King Saul. With Samuel for his constant adviser and friend, with the promises of God sealing the selection of him from the whole people, coming as it were into the place of God as immediate ruler of the nation, not only was he free, but he enjoyed marvellous helps in being good. Upon his transgression, Samuel said to him, " Thou hast done foolishly; — for now would the Lord have established thy kingdom upon Israel forever." To us it is the same as though God had no secret purposes. Yet shall we disallow in him that which merchants and statesmen covet, — prescience? Must God have no purposes and plans, lest that should seem to control the creature's freedom?

———

Peter and Judas in their repentance. — One " went out and wept bitterly "; the other " went out, and it was night."

ONE reason why we enjoy no more in religion may be that we think only of our feelings toward God, and not of his feelings toward us. But "we love him because he first loved us." This should be our expectation,— To receive from God, not merely to give; and therefore we are to seek him with our wants, even more than with our offerings.

PERHAPS God's love of our devotional acts is like our love of microscopic beauty in flowers. At least, their minuteness, compared with the exercises of higher orders of beings, may no more be a reason for his disregard of us, than minuteness is a cause for neglect on the part of a philosopher. There are few optical pleasures greater than the examination of flowers by the aid of an ordinary magnifying-glass. The surface of a common red pink exceeds the glory of Solomon. Fear not "though thou be little."

"AND the seven angels came out of the temple, having the seven plagues, clothed in pure and white linen, and having their breasts girded with golden girdles." Men generally associate angels with birds and flowers. They are executors of God's judgments, as well as ministering spirits. One angel slew a hundred and eighty-five thousand men in one night. Another directed a pestilence in David's time. But more, an angel slew all the first-born of Egypt. God's angels are not after the pattern of our effeminate conceptions. There is no weakness in holiness. "Strength and beauty are in his tabernacle."

THE quiet prayer-meeting at the river's side led to the conversion of Lydia, the imprisonment and release of Paul and Silas, the conversion of the jailer. Never say, "It is only a prayer-meeting."

DO Christians become less zealous as they grow old? They may not be so strong to labor, but it would be one of the most powerful allegations against Christianity, if those who had had longest experience of it should feel and act as though it were a delusion, or did not make good its promises. We must conclude that, while there is the same variety of character among the old as among the younger in the Church of Christ, it is true that

> "His grace will to the end
> Stronger and brighter shine."

We may suppose that the unfeigned faith dwelt as largely in the grandmother Lois as in the mother Eunice. Our observation surely verifies this.

"**H**AST thou not made an hedge about him?" — Satan's observation and reflection with regard to a good man and God's care of him.

INDEPENDENT of parentage, marriage, relationships of any and every kind, the soul has a relation to God which we see and feel when death draws nigh. It asserts itself against father, mother, husband, wife, child. Hence, make most of that relation to God. It was prior to every other; it absorbs them all.

———◆———

EPHRAIM Syrus quaintly represents lambs all over the earth as praising Christ, the Lamb of God, who terminated their appointment for sacrifice. — Hence learn how "the whole creation" will one day partake in the benefits of redemption.

———◆———

TO be kept from certain sins is a proof of God's love. "Whoso pleaseth God shall escape from her; but the sinner shall be taken by her."

LET us be happy in contributing to the sum of human happiness, without ostentation or hope of reward. A teamster has dropped a billet of logwood from his load in the highway. You get no reward for telling him, but you add so much to the welfare of the unknown proprietor; you cheer a laboring man with a gleam of satisfaction.

THOUGH Jesse was blameless, and David's mother is called " thy hand-maid," yet David says, " Behold, I was shapen in iniquity, and in sin did my mother conceive me."

"THERE is a sin not unto death." Then, of course, there is one unto death, or such an exceptional declaration would not have been made. Hence, endless retribution.

THE converse of that passage is true, "As many as I love, I rebuke and chasten." To rebuke and chasten a child makes a parent love him, and in proportion to the good effect of the discipline. So again, God says of Ephraim, "Since I spake against him, I do earnestly remember him still, — I will surely have mercy upon him." Every parent can understand this.

FIFTY-TWO Sabbaths come at the close of a year, stand about you, and say, We are going to the bar of God. We will meet you there. Farewell.

THERE is assimilation of character to the favorite object and chosen good: —

"Whate'er thou lovest, man, that too become thou must;
God, if thou lovest God, dust, if thou lovest dust."

BLOOD must be satisfied. The blood of Christ must be satisfied, by the salvation or punishment of us who shed it. " The voice of thy brother's blood crieth unto me from the ground." So the blood of Christ has a cry. It has cried for eighteen hundred years, and is crying still. It will be satisfied by the travail of his soul. It must be avenged on those who count it an unholy thing.

" HE wakeneth morning by morning."— May God wake us up every day in a right frame. How it cheers and strengthens us for the day to awake in a good frame. Morning thoughts are regarded by us with no little interest. If we begin the night with God, we may hope to say, " When I awake I am still with thee." God will wake us up at the last day. May he now do it, " morning by morning."

O THAT we could have a daily thought of a suffering, dying Saviour! It would keep our hearts tender, our spirits gentle, our words mild, our tempers patient, and make us more loving.

> "Well he remembers Calvary:
> Nor let his saints forget."

———•———

"AND they spake against the God of Jerusalem as against the gods of the people of the earth which were the work of the hands of men." Childlike indignation and reasoning at the affront put upon the Most High.

———•———

"NOW the man out of whom the devils were departed, besought him that he might be with him." O that we might thus cling to Jesus! How safe at his side! Nor will "Satan dare my soul invade."

"Because he could swear by no greater, he sware by himself," — as though He would if He could. And all this effort of protestation to confirm this promise to a believer, — "Surely, blessing I will bless thee, and multiplying I will multiply thee."

"Doth not he see my ways, and count all my steps?" Sometimes how good it is to think of this. As though no one else engaged his attention, God has constant and perfect cognizance of each of us.

Observe this change: "In me, that is, in my flesh, dwelleth no good thing." Now the man who said this was once the straitest of the Pharisees. Self-knowledge is a beautiful and wonderful fruit of regeneration.

"THAT ye may grow thereby." What is a growing Christian? He brings his feelings and conduct more and more to a likeness with those of Christ. He strengthens that in himself which is weak, he puts on certain things which he has not, his aim is increasingly to be like God. He loves the preceptive parts of Scripture. Anything which helps him to know himself, to increase in goodness, is the object of his desire.

———◆———

IT is doubtful if we feel anything very deeply about which we do not speak to others, unless it be unsuitable; and of such things there are very few which we do not find some one to whom we may communicate them. So if we feel much on religious subjects, we shall be ready to talk about them. "I believed, therefore have I spoken; we also believe, and therefore speak."

"I PRAY for them; I pray not for the world, but for those whom thou hast given me." There is a sense in which Christ intercedes for his people as he does not for the world. He must have died for his people with different feelings from those which he had toward others. Christians do not sufficiently think of this. It would increase their sense of obligation to Christ, and awaken confidence and love toward him, to admit this truth. "Particular redemption," as some state it, is not true; yet redemption is particular.

———•———

HERE is demonstration that the Old Testament dispensation was preparatory to the New, instead of the New being an entirely original institution: "I sent you to reap that whereon ye bestowed no labor; other men labored, and ye are entered into their labors." Who were these "other men," if not the Old Testament prophets?

THE expostulations of God (for example, in Amos iv.) show his sincere good-will toward all men. Whatever is true as to his secret purposes, it is equally true that he is sincere in his invitations and promises. These are our rule of duty, not his decrees.

———•———

THAT the moral superiority of all Christians over the heathen is not equal to their intellectual and social superiority, is a proof of the irreparable debasement of human nature. Very many, also, are far better as men and women than they are as Christians.

———•———

THE prosperity of King Uzziah is a wonderful story, 2 Chron. xxvi. The causes which led to it, by the favor of God, are full of admonition and encouragement.

SOME professors of religion seem to subsist on the phenomena of religion. There must be something unusual astir to satisfy them that anything is doing. The Gospel is preached, the lives of men are affected by it, children are taught, cases of conviction and conversion ripen into confirmed hope, one by one, but these Christians must have something new. Sun, moon, and stars are of no account; the comet is all in all. Eyes are turned toward it which never regard the sunrise nor sunset. These Christians are generally less spiritually-minded than others, judging from their prayers.

———◆———

INTELLIGENT men come from their pursuits of ingenuity and industry, and sit and witness the manner in which ministers do their work. With all the acquisitions which they can make of piety and zeal, the ministry must also remember that word to one of their number, "Let no man despise thee."

"THE seed of evil-doers shall never be renowned." Here we have that fearful law of God's administration which connects parent and child through the moral character of the parent. The associations which men have with the memory of an evil-doer involuntarily attach to his child, even where there is no prejudice against the child. Thus God would bring the strongest motives to bear on a parent, seeing that he depends so much for the right ordering of human affairs on the transmitted influence of family religion.

—◆—

"AND in the daytime he was teaching in the temple, and at night he went out and abode in the mount that is called the Mount of Olives." Here was the mixing of retirement and meditation with public service. Continued, uninterrupted reflection and musing for a season, and that frequently, nurtures thought, and gives it strength and freshness.

THAT the only sin which is unpardonable is one committed against the Holy Spirit, should affect us with profound awe toward him. While words are necessary in order to commit that sin, and while no one who has a trembling fear lest he may have committed it can possibly have done so, it must follow, from what is said of the unpardonable sin, that all sins against the Holy Spirit are peculiarly heinous.

DANIEL'S advice to Nebuchadnezzar deserves to be pondered: "Wherefore, O king, let my counsel be acceptable unto thee, and break off thy sins by righteousness, and thine iniquities by showing mercy to the poor." That which was good for the king is good for all. We do well to notice the very frequent connection in the Bible of alms-giving with being accepted of God.

"And the speech pleased the Lord that Solomon had asked this thing." — God is a silent observer of our acts. Some of them give him as true pleasure as they do to a good man who should witness them. To please God is worth constant circumspection and effort.

It is wonderful how a full acceptance of Christ's righteousness by a very wicked man removes his sense of shame. Human society could not do it, even should it heap its honors upon him. But "the blood of Jesus Christ his Son cleanseth us from all sin."

God's ways of treating us are, some of them, a rule and help in our treatment of others. For example, he covers our sins, and does not expose us; is long-suffering; and he is kind to the unthankful.

WE must expend more labor on the Church. Paul worked for it, wrote, prayed for it. It is good soil, it yields returns; it furnishes the instruments by which God will convert the world.

"IF thou cast us out, suffer us to go away into the herd of swine." Were these evil spirits once holy beings? Since God may not be supposed to create demons, these evil spirits had been upright. Behold the change! What end is there to the degradation made by sin? When we fall from God, the pit is bottomless which receives us.

"AND men for thy life." The fall of one and another in the church and ministry is one means of saving us. "And some of them of understanding shall fall, to try and purify and make them white."

"THE old man." Old age is honorable, but "the old man" of whom Paul speaks is an object of aversion. He has the disagreeable peculiarities of age without its beauty and honor. He is obstinate, and peevish, and passionate, and unreasonable, and childish, doting, irresolute, and invincibly attached to his errors and follies, and to his sins. We each have "an old man" in us. With some he is their only nature. Others have also in them "the new man which after God is created in righteousness and true holiness."

"BUT Hezekiah rendered not again according to the benefit done unto him, for his heart was lifted up." We blame him, we wonder at him, we mourn over him, and perhaps go and do likewise. Let us recall past benefits, dwell upon them before God, rehearse his goodness, be as grateful as though these benefits were fresh and new.

"AND the King of Sodom said to Abram, 'Give me the persons, and take the goods to thyself.'" This is also Satan's wish and proposal. He will give us "the goods," provided he may have "the persons."

———◆———

THE Bible is beautifully miscellaneous, like the woods. No methodized, syntactic, prim order, and borders. Every part is perfect, but the connection of the parts has all the lifelike variety of nature.

———◆———

"THE iniquity of the Amorites is not yet full." God thus seems to keep a measure near a wicked man, and the man is filling it. Hence his life is prolonged. So said the Saviour: "Fill ye up, therefore, the measure of your iniquities."

SEEMING success is not real, without God. It may lead to disaster. "For though ye had smitten the whole army of the Chaldeans that fight against you, and there remained but wounded men among them, yet they should rise up every man in his tent, and burn this city with fire." — So failure and disappointment, in God's hands, are frequently doors to great success.

———◆———

"O THOU that hearest prayer, unto thee shall all flesh come"; — for every one, whatever his present feelings, will see a time when he must pray.

———◆———

JOHN mistook a glorified prophet for an angel, Rev. xxii. 8. If departed friends should reappear to us in their heavenly state, we should do the same.

IF we repent, God hereafter makes our sins change to sources of blessing. Judas never can know this. But if we are saved, God will make even our sins turn to good account. They will widen our sympathies with the redeemed, make us appreciate redemption, qualify us for service.

IT is the same as though in heaven the rocks were rending, the sun were darkened, the graves were opened, the Son of God were dying, rising again. The atonement is having effect. Christ is making intercession for us.

NOTICE the coincidence between Cornelius's and Peter's visions. They had the same object, — to bring the two men together. So God is at work for us in different places at the same time. "How precious, also, are thy thoughts unto me, O God."

EVERY Communion Sabbath the same reproach may be laid against the Saviour at his table, as when he was on earth, — "This man receiveth sinners, and eateth with them." But are they who now utter this reproach Pharisees, as formerly?

"HE that made him can make his sword to approach unto him." These words, spoken of Behemoth, we may apply to a seemingly incorrigible sinner, to a cruel enemy, to an unfeeling creditor, to an unnatural relative.

THE book of the Law was sprinkled with blood, showing two things; — 1. God's justice is satisfied by the atonement; 2. Our obedience is accepted only through the sacrifice of Christ.

HOW little do we feel that we have been pardoned. We rather feel that once we were unhappy, and now have hope. But we are released convicts, escaped criminals, ransomed captives, who had sold themselves. Should we sin so easily, if we remembered that we have had a just, eternal punishment remitted?

———•———

"FOR they cannot recompense thee." On doing good for its own sake, selecting cases where it seems impossible that we should get any returns for it in this world. Yet how rare that a good deed is not discovered. "But thou shalt be recompensed at the resurrection of the just." We are tempted to say, Would that we might be allowed to do some good without being recompensed. Yet we must be. It is a law of the moral universe. It cannot be prevented, for those helpless ones whom we benefit here will blazon it in heaven. And what can we do?

"THIS is the message which we have heard of Him," — but what can it be, announced with such emphasis? Simply this, — "that God is light, and in him is no darkness at all." It seems, at first, almost a truism; but reflect, and ponder it. Things seem dark to us, but not to Him. Were there no darkness in us, there would be no unbelief, no jealousies, hatred, no secret sins.

———♦———

THERE surely is that in God which in man we should call Humility; as, for example, in his being willing to institute a comparison between himself and idols. We can hardly speak of them and of him together without some sense of impropriety. But the Most High frequently enters into an argument with Israel as to his superiority to blocks of wood and stone.

HAMAN and the horse, — this almost silly choice among offered royal gifts. He verifies that common name of a sinner in the Bible, — fool. Perhaps when every sinner and his choice are made public, the term will be seen to be equally just. Some young men will do well to think of this, especially in their Sabbath recreations.

———◆———

"AND now men see not the bright light which is in the clouds; but the wind passeth and cleanseth them"; — that is, Afflictive dispensations are inwardly bright, and are easily removed by a word from God.

———◆———

TRUTHFULNESS must pervade the whole character. "Behold, thou desirest truth in the inward parts."

"TAKE a cheerful view of these words: 'Let your moderation be known unto all men; the Lord is at hand.'" Not merely coming to judgment; but, at hand to help, to avenge you; hence be not disquieted; moderate your resentments, your fears, your despondency.

"IT may be God will requite me good for his cursing." We take part with an injured person, and the weaker side. God acts on every good principle which prevails among men.

"AND she bare him Aaron and Moses." What a father and mother! Why were two such sons conferred on one family! God is sometimes affluent in gifts of one and the same kind. He is "able to do exceeding abundantly above all that we ask or think."

"AND being in an agony, he prayed more earnestly"; "And he said, Abba, Father." — Agony made him more filial, more loving, more conscious of the Father's relation to him.

THINK of Christ as having common, practical views of things; not as a sentimentalist and pietist. He cannot be deceived, nor be satisfied with our frames and professions, when our principles and conduct are not good.

WE are apt to think and speak of good men in the Bible as though they were not sinners like us; whereas they had the same frailties; and their confessions of sin exceed ours. We know their evil deeds, but suppose that the private histories of those who speak against them were known.

CHRIST'S reply to one who invoked a blessing on his mother, shows that there is no prescriptive claim to eminence in his kingdom, not even by being mother to Jesus. Goodness alone opens the way, and that is sure, and is in no danger of being superseded, or turned aside by accident of birth.

A DEAR Christian friend said to me, "I never overhear one praying without feeling impelled to pray for him, that his prayer may be answered." Blessed Intercessor and Advocate! this is the case with Thee, whenever our voice in prayer reaches thine ear.

"SURELY he hath borne our griefs." — Christ saw this trouble before I felt it. His heart was pierced by it before it pierced mine.

JOB'S scorn (ch. xxx.). Paul and Silas's spirited reply to the rulers who had imprisoned them. John's detestation of heretics. Jude's denunciation of false teachers, and his description of their end. — But it is easier to imitate these right things in good men, than their humility and meekness.

ANGELS met Jacob, not at the moment of need, but to prepare him for it. Our religious opportunities, in times of health and strength, are like these angels. Let us know the day of our visitation.

WHEN baffled in our meditations upon the being of God, it is good to know that it was a truly devout man who said, " Touching the Almighty, we cannot find him out."

THE first ear of corn, bunch of grapes, and early fruit of any kind, awakens a strange delight. "That we should be a kind of first-fruits of his creatures." James i. 18. It looks as though redeemed men would be such, in the view of other beings, owing to the infinite cost at which we have been produced in this most unpromising and once accursed field.

———◆———

THE Holy Spirit looked down through time to this very morning, and saw you in need of a word to instruct, comfort, or guide you. He caused Jabez, or Manasseh, or Hosea, or Paul, to say something, so many centuries ago, which should serve you to-day. So of every Christian, through time.

———◆———

IN Christ, we are as safe at the bar of God as Christ would be.

THE place and use of Fear in religion.— It is a rebuke to those who make fondness the principal element in piety, that the chief exponent of religion is "the fear of the Lord." One whose piety is in danger of being too soft and flaccid will do well to read Cruden's Concordance, under the word *Fear*, and its various connected uses.

THINKING of dying, it seems unspeakably desirable to have begun in childhood to fear and serve the glorious Lord God. "Remember now thy Creator, in the days of thy youth."

"FOLLOW peace with all men, and holiness," &c. Is a connection intimated here between these things? Surely one is a means to the other, and indispensable to it.

"THEY came to the iron gate, which opened to them of his own accord." Beautiful fiction, as though a celestial hand were not moving it. And yet, things being described in the Bible as they appear, it is strictly true. So do inflexible circumstances change, and insuperable hinderances move out of the way, when God is at work for us.

GREAT and awful judgments were inflicted at the opening of the Gospel, on Ananias and Sapphira, Elymas, &c., with a view, no doubt, to give the impression that the Gospel was not intended as a truce to sin.

"I WILL be a God to thee." What must this be? He is not *a God* to the wicked, any more than lightning is nature.

"NOW, therefore, put away Ashtaroth," &c. Some favored sin is the cause of every departure from God, and lies at the foundation of an impenitent state. In every case of impenitence, the renunciation of some particular sin would powerfully help toward regeneration.

INSTEAD of David being peculiar in the use of imprecations, as we might be led to suppose from common remarks about him, what sacred writer does not use them, or quote them?

ISRAEL could not drive out the inhabitants of the plain (Judges i.) because they had "chariots of iron." Yet God was with Judah. True, but He would not always work miracles. Here is an instance of Divine power regarding the natural force of circumstances.

EVEN when the Mediatorship is ended, the enlightening and guiding influences of the Holy Spirit, which are not in their nature temporary, but belong to his Divine nature, will no doubt be employed for the advancement of redeemed souls in knowledge forever. And so that gratitude, which now we owe him for every good thought and right feeling, will swell to a boundless debt, till our love toward him may not be exceeded even by our love to the Redeemer. Notice a word used by Paul in connection with the Holy Spirit, and also the recognition of the Sacred Three in one verse: "Now I beseech you for the Lord Jesus Christ's sake, and for the love of the Spirit, that ye strive together in your prayers to God for me."

BALAAM, Gehazi, Judas, Ananias, were not recovered, while others were. What was the one sin of those men? Covetousness.

A SHORT crop in this country deranges the finances. No country is more immediately dependent on God than we. But what a responsibility it is to take charge of suns, and showers, and winds, day by day and at the same time to rule the cabinets, and plan for you and make your little child well of fever, and hear your prayers and put your tears into his bottle. What a God! who would sin against Him? "O that men would praise the Lord for his goodness, and for his wonderful works to the children of men!"

———•———

HOW free the Israelites were with their offerings when a false god was to be made! So men are free and lavish in their amusements, their pleasures, their dress, dwellings, and equipage, and backward in the cause of Christian benevolence, until their love to God reaches the same level with their former love of self.

HAD not the translators left some passages obscure, and perhaps equivocal, each sect would have had its Bible. Now all can put their own interpretation on those places. The Bible is thus like a portrait, which seems to every one in the room to be looking specially at him.

———◆———

THE last words of God on Sinai to Moses (Exodus xxxi.) had reference to the observance of the Sabbath. After a long interview, and when we have given instructions to one who is to serve us, the thing which we dwell upon just at parting, repeating it with special emphasis, is a thing to which we attach great importance.

———◆———

"THE world" has no "Comforter." (John xiv. 17.)

"FOR he seeth wickedness also; will he not then consider it?" We meditate and dwell on a base act, analyze it, and constantly abhor it. What if God thus dwells upon our acts of evil-doing? Sometimes he makes us feel that he does so. Thus David: "Thou hast set our iniquities before thee, our secret sins in the light of thy countenance."

NO one, probably, was ever disappointed at finding himself in heaven. Many have been and will be disappointed in not finding themselves there.

WHAT constitutes covetousness? We need to know; for is there more said against any one sin, or said in stronger terms, in the New Testament, than against this?

"AND he took of the stones of the place and set them up for his pillow, and lay down in that place to sleep." So we may do everywhere and always, — the circumstances of every condition, no matter how unforbidding and repulsive, affording us always, if we will, a source of rest and consolation.

———◆———

HERE I am on the shore of the sea. What if the sea were veiled, and I had never beheld it, and yet had often walked on its coasts. So the invisible world, and that "ocean we must sail so soon," lie close at hand, concealed.

———◆———

MARK, writing under directions from Peter, omits to praise him as the other Evangelists indirectly do; but he gives his faults most fully.

AFTER talking with one who was anxious about his spiritual state, but with no fixed belief of anything, and seemingly incapable of coherent views of things, I have been instructed by seeing men drive piles into a loose soil. The object is to get one pile at a time firmly fixed. So we should aim to fix some one truth in the mind, and it is comparatively of little consequence what the truth is, the object being simply to excite faith.

ONE great error of the Perfectionists is this: They expect to get into *a state*, — a state in which they will not sin. One was probably saved from that delusion by asking her, one wintry day, if she ever expected to get into a state of not slipping on the ice? — The Christian life is a slippery way up to the very gate of the heavenly city, and even while entering. "Hold thou me up, and I shall be safe."

"MY covenant was with him (Levi) of life and peace." Mal. ii. 5. God's covenant with ministers. When they are right and good, they must be a great joy to Him who chooses to work by instruments, and "has need" of these laborers, "workers together with God." They may expect covenant blessings.

TAKE salvation as freely as you would buy it, if you had the means, or as you would buy any worldly commodity. "Ho every one that thirsteth, — and he that hath no money, — come ye, — buy, —without money."

PERFECTNESS under an administration of grace is consistent with indwelling sin, strong temptations, lapses, in short, with being imperfect, the individual being sincerely a follower of Christ.

JOAB directed his main attack against the auxiliar force, 1 Chron. xix. This was good generalship. They had no homes and country there to fight for, and could be more easily discomfited, and the effect of routing them would be to dismay the Syrians. The Bible is rich in its incidental instructions. Was a man ever in circumstances to which there is nothing corresponding in the Bible?

———◆———

IN religion, " pietism," that is, frames, emotions, meditative religion, — very beautiful often, but without activity, — corresponds to that which in painting is called " still-life."

———◆———

WELL might the Saviour sing at the Supper, looking beyond those few following days.

THERE must have been more appearances of Christ in the Old Testament than we usually find, judging from the frequent mention, in the New Testament, of his agency under the old dispensation.

———◆———

PAUL came to Troas, and found a wide door opened to him, but had no rest because he found not Titus his brother. We love him for this touch of innocent weakness. So he beseeches Timothy to do diligence, and come to him, telling who had forsaken him.

———◆———

WAS Paul ever "forsaken" by any? Did any leave his ministry for insufficient reasons? We are glad to know it, if it were so. (2 Tim. iv. 10, 16.)

NOTICE the unstudied, but wonderful expressions about Christ, in the prophets and in the New Testament. They drop without system, are mostly incidental, yet each is beyond explanation unless Christ be divine, and all together they have that peculiar power which cumulative evidence has on a jury, the weightier for being somewhat disjoined, and without concert.

REPRESENTATIVE guilt and punishment appear in these words: — "That on you may come all the righteous blood from Abel."

"HEARKEN, and serve the King of Babylon." Humiliating word! So, submit to chastisement, mortifying, bitter to pride, if God clearly appoints it.

THE " three " who appeared to Abraham, as he sat in his tent-door, we do not suppose had designed reference to the Three that bear record in heaven ; yet do Christians ever have any experience of communion with those " Three " together ? Why not ? Christ says, " My Father will love him, and we will come unto him, and make our abode with him." O never-to-be-forgotten experience, if, in some season of great sorrow or trial, you had a sense of being visited by the Sacred Three !

———◆———

GOD appeals to the mountains as judges between him and his people, Micah vi. Beautiful condescension to our habits of thought. He is willing to leave the case to referees. We have very limited conceptions of the gentleness of God. The passages which bring it to view are chiefly in the Old Testament. A rejoinder, here, to allegations against that book.

A COMMON idea with many of being "an excellent Christian" is, to be kind to the poor, upright, obliging, courteous;— leaving out of the case a work of God upon the heart. But many who have this work have all these moral and social qualities also.

TO be baptized in the name of the Holy Spirit, to be blessed in his name in the Christian benediction, as really prove his personality and deity, as baptism and benediction prove the personality of the Father.

AND some believed the words which were spoken, and some believed not." Acts (last chapter). It is very much so when other ministers than Paul reason and preach. Let them not be disheartened.

THE inspection of a single bone will sometimes enable the comparative anatomist to describe in general the structure of an unknown animal. There are passages of Scripture having no connection with any argument for a system, which reveal a system, or some fundamental truth. For example, Paul says to the Galatians, "Was Paul crucified for you?" Here is a recognition, the more impressive for its being incidental, of the vicarious sacrifice of Christ. Here is another instance: "Destroy not him with thy meat for whom Christ died."

"WHEREFORE askest thou after my name, seeing it is secret?" Consider the value and beauty of privacy in religion, as regards some experiences which never can be mentioned without both breaking a certain charm in them to ourselves, and incurring the suspicion of fanaticism, or at least presumption.

"THE Lord hath set apart him that is godly for himself." We look with interest upon the article which the manufacturer of some rare and valuable product, or upon the lot of land which a land proprietor, has set apart for himself. No godly person escapes the eye of God. "The Lord's portion is his people." "Israel is his peculiar inheritance."

TO be melancholy after confession and repentance implies a want of faith in God. "Be of good cheer, thy sins are forgiven thee."

REPENTANCE is the sorrow of love. It is doubtful whether we ever repent towards any one till touched with some gentle emotion toward him. Is it not so with repentance toward God?

"QUESTIONING with themselves what the rising from the dead should mean." Reading the bold, clear arguments of the Apostles on that subject, it is encouraging to think of their early ignorance, and to see how the course of events and experience will instruct and advance those who thirst for Christian knowledge.

"IF he were on earth, he would not be a priest." But why?—Because his own death and blood invested him with the priestly office.—Here we have an indirect testimony to the sacrificial nature of our Saviour's character and office.

CHRIST lay in the grave the whole of the Jewish Sabbath, but the whole of no other day.

"THE kings of the earth, and all the inhabitants of the world, would not have believed that the adversary and the enemy should have entered into the gates of Jerusalem." Lam. iv. 12. So ministers, and professed Christians of eminent reputation, may astonish others by their perdition. God will show his infinite greatness by his independence of the greatest of men and of angels.

ON being guileless. "Behold an Israelite indeed, in whom is no guile." — Yet Nathaniel was only a man; sinful man, therefore, can secure such approbation from Christ.

DANIEL charged Belshazzar with two things: 1. Not improving by his father's sins and punishment; 2. Not glorifying God.

GOD sees our imperfections more than we. "Faithful are the wounds of a friend." That enemy of yours was employed by God to tell you a cutting but needful truth. Turn away your resentment, and be grateful to God for letting you see yourself. The prayer you uttered a month or two since, "Search me, O God, and know my heart," has just now been answered in this reproach, this backbiting, this bitter enmity.

WARNINGS are ineffectual in themselves. We would have supposed that the fall of Judas would have made the eleven disciples keep closer to Christ, instead of forsaking him, or following afar off.

HOPELESS deaths: "And Aaron held his peace."

WE are honored in having no lower standard proposed to us than perfection, God himself. "Be ye therefore perfect, even as your Father in heaven is perfect." This sometimes excites querulous remarks, as though it were severe, an impossible exaction. But it should be our glory and joy. How would we have it? Shall the best of men, or angels, be our standard? No; God is the goal after which we are to aspire.

"WHAT continuance hath an image in a glass, if the man turn away his face?" So if God withdraw, what becomes of his image in our souls? Angelic perfection is only a creature. How far our native corruption will work if it be irritated, and God suspends the influence of his grace, we may have seen in the case of others, but the greatest illustration of it we shall find in our own temptations.

"NOT by water only, but by water and blood." We cannot be saved by outward washings, reformations, observances. Blood must atone for our sins. We cannot be saved merely by being good, and we cannot be saved without it. "By water and blood."

———◆———

OBLIGATION is not to be measured by moral ability; for then there would be as many standards as there are individuals and their degrees of ability. There is one standard for all, and that is God. Our moral impotence does not change it, nor lessen its obligation.

———◆———

"THE High-Priest asked Jesus of his disciples." What an inquiry just at that time, and under those circumstances.

"AND God hath both raised up the Lord, and will also raise up us by his own power." Here is identification of the believer with Christ; a parallelism of our resurrection and that stupendous event, — the resurrection of Christ. Notice the act of God, the Father, in raising us from the dead, while it is also the frequently asserted prerogative of Christ.

SUPPOSE that Christ had stood for us instead of Adam, as our federal head? How safe we should have been. He has stood for us, our second Adam. How safe we are in him.

"ALL things were made by him and for him," — namely, these relationships, these affections, these talents and opportunities, as well as those planetary worlds.

DO not always dwell on "ability" in the sinner. "Blessed art thou, Simon Barjona; for flesh and blood hath not revealed it unto thee, but my Father which is in heaven." Set men to search and pray for things which, with all their ability, they must receive as free gifts to the undeserving.

―――――♦―――――

"THOU art weighed in the balances." Our sins will go into the same side of the balance with the law of God, to weigh against us. But what if Christ and his righteousness be counted on our part against them?

―――――♦―――――

DANIEL did not call Belshazzar to repentance, as he did Nebuchadnezzar. His doom was fixed. His sin was unto death. "I do not say that he shall pray for it."

THE Saviour taking those three men to watch at the gate of Gethsemane while he suffered, teaches us the use and the true way of showing sympathy to the afflicted. We all crave it; so did Christ. Draw near to the afflicted. It was that which Christ desired, and not much speaking.

NO doubt whole households will here and there be seen in the world of sin and suffering,— father, mother, brother, sister, having made that unprofitable gain of the world for the soul, and now losing both.

NOAH'S ark in itself was a "vain thing for safety." Putting to sea in it in such a flood was safe only because the covenant of God made it so.

WE must not expect sorrows and sufferings as unmitigated attendants upon growing old. To many aged people we have seen that word fulfilled in their serene or even joyful frames of mind: "And thine age shall be clearer than the noonday."

———◆———

"LOVE his appearing." Wicked servants and children do not love the sudden appearing of the master and father. But to love the appearing of Christ is one characteristic, mentioned in the New Testament, of Christians.

———◆———

BOAZ on his sheaves, his heart merry with wine, and with Ruth at his feet, unknown to him, is a picture of happiness approaching one whom God has designed to bless.

WE cannot express the direct and indirect help which we have derived in trouble from passages of Scripture. We think in them, in a large measure, — they seem to be the currency of our minds at such times. "This is my comfort in my affliction, for thy word hath quickened me."

―――♦―――

CHRIST atoned on Calvary for all those sins which now trouble your conscience. Now you endure some of the consequences of those sins, but the guilt of them was atoned for. Go in peace, in view of this.

―――♦―――

SUPPOSE that this and that individual, whom we can name, should meet us in hell? Let us imagine the interview, have a good conscience toward him now, and flee from the wrath to come.

IT is noticeable that, after such striking events as preceded Samson's birth, his life and death should have been so full of painful conflict; but he is mentioned with honor, in Hebrews xi., among those who by faith gained a good report. If God honors us or our children with early signs of his favor, it may be that we and they may suffer for him. But then we shall glorify him.

———◆———

HE had risen, he had been in heaven, he had finished the work of redemption, and yet this infinite Redeemer meets a company of weary and hungry friends on the sea-shore, and having with his own hands kindled a fire and laid fish thereon, he says to them, "Come and dine." Condescending Friend! no service for us is beneath thee. Common blessings are all thy gifts. Thou wouldst wash the feet of every friend of thine, if it were necessary.

SEE how they marked off and parcelled out Canaan, yet unconquered. "By faith they subdued kingdoms." One king had nine hundred chariots of iron. What of this? He too was marked out for conquest. So let us lay out plans of usefulness, seek the conversion of individuals, benefit classes of people, attempt reformations, notwithstanding discouragements and opposition, and seek to conquer the world for Christ.

———◆———

WE have afflicted God with our sins more than he ever afflicted us by trials. "Thou hast wearied me with thine iniquities."

———◆———

WHEN tempted, fall to praying, and Satan, rather than do you so much good, will desist. Thus "resist the devil, and he will flee from you."

CONSIDERING the pre-existence of fallen angels and their history, the first mention of them in the Bible is beautifully simple, and in accordance with the Divine plan not to disclose things prematurely. "Now *the serpent* was more subtle than any beast of the field which the Lord God had made, and *he* said unto the woman," &c. Had the existence and agency of fallen spirits been directly asserted, it would have made explanations necessary which would have been out of place in the chronology of revelation.

"ASLEEP on a pillow." It was a deliberate sleep. He had not sunk down accidentally; but though he knew the storm was coming, he took a pillow and went to sleep. When we have done our duty, and nothing remains for us to do, we may safely commit all to God, and take our rest in safety.

IT would be difficult to mention a class of individuals to whom something in the Saviour's life does not apply. It is pleasant to think that, by his unseen direction, the thirty pieces of silver for which he was betrayed were appropriated to buy a strangers' burying-place. O ye who wander over the earth feeling homeless and desolate, consider that Jesus thought of the stranger and the homeless, and identified them with one of the intensely interesting events connected with his sufferings and death. One of his specifications to the righteous in his approval of them at the final judgment is, "For I was a stranger and ye took me in."

"HE is able to subdue all things unto himself"; — those hard cases of irreligion, that opposition, all this wealth and talent, this whole population. Therefore pray, labor, wait, and do not "make haste."

"THOU art the God that doest wonders." And these wonders will never cease. We are repeatedly surprised by them, and we shall be. Things will not proceed according to our low and feeble measures. We are to expect great things while God reigns, "who only doeth wondrous things." They will be in proportion to our humble, consistent, patient faith. "Said I not unto thee," said Jesus to Martha, at her brother's grave, "that if thou wouldest believe, thou shouldest see the glory of God?"

———

ON becoming a Christian, we convert everything into a friend and helper, whereas before everything was liable to be against us. A sinner's conscience gives him constant alarm and pain till its voice is silenced. But on becoming a Christian, he invokes its aid : —

> "Conscience, whom I with opiates plied,
> Now wake and be my faithful guide."

"HAVING food and raiment, let us be therewith content." A small inventory of possessions. But there is nothing else which may not be a source of annoyance and sorrow. If God gives us more, let us receive it, but only as stewards, and not build our happiness upon it. — One of our richest men told his confidential clerk, when he applied for the place, that the wages would be his food and clothing. In reply to his remonstrance, the rich man said, "That is all which I ever received from my whole property."

"HOWBEIT, not all that came out of Egypt by Moses." Is it possible that, after such experience, any of them could fail of the promised land? Then we will not presume upon our supposed conversion, nor upon the signs of God's favor in times past, but continually labor to enter into that rest.

NOTICE some gentle rebukes of unbelief; for example: Moses was not commanded to smite the rock the second time, but simply to speak to it. Again, Samuel did not sacrifice a thousand oxen when he would assure Israel of Divine help against Philistia; he offered " a sucking lamb."

THE spoils of Samaria, gathered after the retreat of its army, and during a famine in Jerusalem, show the unthought-of ways in which God can come to our relief in the greatest extremity. " Trust in him at all times."

HERE is a prescription of holy writ in cases of despondency: " O my God, my soul is cast down within me; therefore I will remember thee." What could be better?

THERE are many instructions to be gathered from the words of Christ which are profitable in the formation of character and the guidance of conduct, though not essential to salvation. For example, He inculcates modesty: "When thou art bidden of any man to a feast," &c. He admonishes us to act in secret, under the apprehension that our most private words and deeds may be known. "Whatsoever is spoken in the ear," &c. He teaches us to consider the incapacity of some to appreciate our good things, and so not to cast our pearls before swine. An obliging disposition, a readiness to do a kind act, are enjoined by the general rule, "Give to him that asketh of thee," &c.

IF God takes away earthly objects, however important and dear, that he may himself fill the vacant places, he honors you. "Let him do what seemeth him good."

"GOD left him, to try him, that he might know all that was in his heart." So with us: and all through life the painful lessons which we thereby learn keep us humble, make us watchful, and are among the most powerful means of insuring our salvation.

SELECT one of the many specifications in the Saviour's injuries at his trial, and during the time preceding and following, and dwell upon it. For example, "And the servants did strike him with the palms of their hands."

THE interview between Jesus and his mother after his resurrection is not recorded. One might almost say, that the inspiration of the Bible is as clearly seen in that which is omitted as in its actual contents.

ON the arrival of some great event, some emergency, some critical and all-important turn in your affairs, you cannot pray. The mind is too much excited for anything more than ejaculations. They are heard; but how good it is, then, to reflect that, while there were no excitements, you maintained prayer and walked with God, irrespective of passing events. Now he will " reward thee openly."

———◆———

"AND the ruin of that house was great." It might have been " a habitation of God through the Spirit." Christ was often seen at its door; the Holy Spirit was often heard within striving with some one to do him good; blessings from heaven arrived there without number; it was filled " with pleasant riches"; it might have been an eternal habitation. But it fell, "and great was the fall of it."

FROM what sins is Christ saving me? "He shall save his people from their sins." Not merely from their future consequences. Nor is his object merely to give us hope. Hence you who despond because your hope is feeble, repent, forsake sin, believe, be redeemed from all iniquity. This was the purpose of Christ's death, and not merely to give you a comfortable expectation of heaven.

"HE went down to Capernaum, he and his mother and his brethren and his disciples; and they continued there not many days." It was a pleasant gathering; it must have been a heaven on earth! But rest, and those rich enjoyments, were, for him, "not many days." He must be about his Father's business. We have snatches of bliss here in our meetings with Christian friends; but this is not our rest.

A TRANSLATOR and a commentator ought to be men of faith. Otherwise the words of inspiration passing through their minds are robbed of their beautiful freedom, and come to us in a cold and rigid shape. There is an artlessness in inspiration which a man of mere exactness, and, much more, a doubting man, utterly destroys. It is painful to read his translations and comments.

A FIELD of tall, ripe grain, bowing under a gentle wind, looks like a great worshipping host, under one and the same impulse of heavenly joy. Each of those stalks has its root, its distinct organization, its full number of grains; it has enjoyed the culture of the husbandman and the sweet influences of the heavens. God has done as much for it as for its neighbor, knows it as well; and a part of its duty and service in return is to make one in a harvest-field.

"HOWL, fir-tree, for the cedar is fallen." The removal of great and good men from posts of usefulness, when they are succeeded by inferior and unworthy men, is a divine judgment. "And I will give children to be their princes, and babes shall rule over them."

ACTING on coincidences without judgment, and seeing providences without due reflection, is as bad as trusting to dreams. We may get useful hints from dreams, but they are not our guide. Wisdom and discretion must judge as to the inferences to be drawn from them.

ESCAPES from imminent danger have an effect sometimes on good people to make them feel safe. God was there.

WAS it accidental or designed, that Paul, in addressing the two ministers, Timothy and Titus, should add "mercy" to the "grace and peace" with which he addressed every Church to whom his Epistles are directed? To these he says, "Grace be unto you and peace"; but to the ministers he says, "Grace, mercy, and peace." Peter also says, "Grace and peace," only, to Christians. We ministers specially need the "mercy," — from others, for our mistakes, and our incapacity; and from God, for our sins, which must be worse than those of others.

THE selection of Canaan for "the Holy Land," the Arab race, and other things related thereto, are striking illustrations of the providence of God coinciding with seemingly fixed inevitable laws and events, as though all were not originally designed and made expressly for the purposes of Redemption.

WHAT impression may the Bible be fairly said to have made on the world as to essential truths? what, amidst and underneath all that is denominational and sectarian, do we find to be accepted by all who receive the Bible as "the word of God"? On every principle of common sense those truths are the truths of God's word.

REPENTANCE is impossible where there is no atonement for sin. This is capable of a strong argument. The bearing of this truth on the future condition of the wicked, when there shall be "no more sacrifice for sin," is obvious.

IF wicked men could have the Most High in their power, it is not difficult to see what they would do with him.

THE thought of never coming back to this world, of leaving it at once and forever, is deeply affecting. We shall be glad if it be better for our having lived in it. "The world and all that is therein shall be burnt up." Even if we inhabit this globe again, we shall recognize nothing, if everything shall have been burnt up. Now is our time to work for the good of the world.

———◆———

THE penitent thief had a better righteousness in which to appear before God than the most accomplished moralist in the Sanhedrim.

———◆———

WHAT a good kingdom this must be, of which it is said, it "is not meat and drink, but righteousness, and peace, and joy in the Holy Ghost."

SEE the natural connection here: "Full of goodness, filled with all knowledge, able, also, to admonish one another." We do not willingly suffer one to occupy this last position, unless he answers to the first two parts of the description. All such are gladly listened to when they admonish.

———◆———

DREAMS will no doubt be surpassed hereafter by realities; some of them exquisitely pleasurable and others inconceivably dreadful. "Dull sleep instructs, nor sport vain dreams in vain."

———◆———

BE reverent in all expressions of love to God; for forms of speech are defences against improprieties. The Saviour is our example and pattern in addressing God.

CHRIST was to Adam a man, to Abraham a Hebrew, to Moses a prophet, to Isaiah a man of sorrows, to David a king, to Daniel a suffering, sacrificed Messiah. There is a progression, now, in the minds of many respecting Christ. Let them not be discouraged. "Unto you that fear my name shall the Sun of righteousness arise with healing in his wings; and ye shall go forth, and grow up like calves of the stall."

WHEN the end of a trial is evidently near, we see how easy it is for God to clear the darkest skies; we generally find that all has happened in the best time; we are sorry at impatience; we perhaps feel grateful for the subduing and softening influence of the trial, and we may well fear lest with relief we forget God. "The Lord will speak peace unto his people and to his saints; but let them not turn again to folly."

THE Saviour went three times into Gethsemane on that night of his agony. We must not expect that a single prayer of ours, or one effort, will accomplish any great thing for our souls or for the souls of others. The Saviour came back from Gethsemane with these words on his lips, — a result of his experience there: "Watch and pray that ye enter not into temptation."

WHEN David saw that the Lord had answered him in the threshing-floor of Ornan, he sacrificed to him there. We do well to identify our acknowledgments of God's goodness with the places and times of his bestowments.

NEW YEAR. How much God has to do for you this year! Begin it with him.

ON revisiting places, where God was good to us, in preserving, helping, comforting, and in various ways blessing us. "And let us arise and go up to Bethel, and I will make there an altar unto God, who answered me in the day of my distress, and was with me in the way which I went." Sadness in memory of the past should not keep us from doing this.

IN great bodily pain or mental distress, we are instructed how to vent our groans, and on whom to call, by these words of the Most High: "And they have not cried unto me with their heart when they howled upon their beds."

FANCY yourself with men of the Bible, comparing your opportunities with theirs.

THEY who love and worship the Holy Spirit are deeply interested in the belief of judicious critics, that by the " seven spirits which are before his throne," is designated some infinite mystery concerning the Holy Spirit, concerning which, indeed, it is in vain to inquire, but the unfolding of which hereafter will excite our wonder and love with regard to him beyond expression.

———◆———

"AND they took Dagon and set him in his place again." Men sometimes repeat the sins and follies for which they had been signally humbled and chastised.

———◆———

HEIRS of heaven get a larger " earnest of their inheritance" than heirs of rich men.

IT is a beautiful illustration of the nature of faith, that, though we speak so often to God, and Christ, and the Holy Spirit, and have no audible or sensible reply, we continue to pray. We should not long address a fellow-creature without some response. But we are answered, and are made to feel that we are;—not always at the time of praying,—for that might weaken faith.

IF you so love Christ whom you have not seen, how must it be when you see him? Your eternity is to be an eternity of loving and being loved.

"AND a great company of the priests were obedient to the faith." We must not despair of conversions among the ecclesiastics of erroneous systems.

THE key note of preaching should be Salvation, as it is that of the Gospel, and all we say should be governed accordingly. "For God hath not appointed us to wrath, but to obtain salvation through our Lord Jesus Christ."

"FOR none might enter into the king's gate clothed in sackcloth." Esther iv. 2. Would that we could spiritualize this rule at the gate of mercy and at the gate of the Lord's house.

JOSEPH was two years old or less when his mother died. He surely could not have succeeded better in life had she lived to train him. God does not need even a mother in fulfilling his gracious purposes to a child of his covenanted love.

"ECCLESIASTES" is, much of it, the moody reflections of a man troubled with the mysteries of Divine Providence. Some passages in the writings of the able and eloquent John Foster remind one of this book. Parnell's "Hermit" may profitably be read on this subject.

―――♦―――

THERE is only one affection in which there is no danger of excess, and that is Love to God. Everything else may be inordinate and hurtful; but that which is best of all may be indulged without limitation or fear.

―――♦―――

INTOLERANCE is laid down by the Apostle as a sign of being in the wrong. "But as then he that was born after the flesh persecuted him that was born after the Spirit, even so it is now."

EVERY future hour will have its own duty, sorrow, care; how then can you postpone the duty of the present hour, which is, to repent, and so burden a future hour with it, which will be sufficiently occupied with its own urgent concern? Men of business know how wrong this is in their private affairs.

SEE the effect of one angel on the Roman guard at the tomb of Christ. "And for fear of him the keepers did shake, and became as dead men." Hence, when "the Son of Man shall come in his glory, and all the holy angels with him," well is it said, "then shall he sit upon the throne of his glory."

BE "wise to do good." Invent ways, create means, find subjects.

"AND had a wall great and high." All these emblems of heaven must of course be in keeping with the nature of the place. If so, it may properly be asked, What need of a wall round about heaven, if heaven be not in any sense exclusive? Whom will there be to shut out, if all are saved? And if all are saved, why need they be shut in?

WHENEVER we detect any evil thing in us, let us act toward it as we do toward an eruption, or a disease, or a damage threatening the house.

THE Holy Spirit made the Bible for his chief instrument in his official work. He took sixteen centuries in which to do it, from Moses to John.

THERE are many commands in the Old Testament from God himself to love Him, — not invitations, nor permissions, nor exhortations, but commands, enforced by the most solemn injunctions and penalties. This may be a relief to those who fear to approach God with their affections.

———

WHAT if, ages hence, we should be summoned, for the first time, to eat the flesh and drink the blood of Him whom we shall have known as our final Judge. What a sacrament that would be! We do it now, in anticipation. What a sacrament this will hereafter seem to have been!

———

DEATH made Pharaoh give up his bondmen and his jewels.

SOME who are convinced and persuaded neglect, and sometimes refuse, to make a Christian profession, for the reason that a friend is believed to have died without a Christian hope. To embrace a certain faith will seem to be a condemnation of the friend. "If he is lost, I prefer to be lost with him!" Perhaps, however, in his last hours, unknown to you, he accepted that Gospel which you, for his sake, reject, and so he may be saved, and you, by loving him more than Christ, may be forever separated from both.

THE life of Christ was a life of incidents. Let us be willing that ours should be so, meeting each as he did. Then we shall always have something to do, and be saved from that aimless, listless condition which is the bane of Christian character and usefulness. We shall also be kept from uselessly looking out for some great good to accomplish.

"AND he took the blind man by the hand, and led him out of the town." Perhaps the excitement of being cured in public would have been inconsistent with the circumstances of the patient. If so, see the Divine regard to circumstances, even in a miracle. We must regard means, and adapt ourselves to circumstances, not relying on Divine power for preternatural help. When this blind man was cured, he was sent to his own house, and was forbidden to go into the town. If we neglect the use of proper means, we must cast no blame on God.

"THY gentleness hath made me great." God knows how to encourage, to help us on, "gently lead" us; whereas harshness and violence, with impatience, frustrate the best designs. The Bible has the only true standard and rules of education. It is a book for parents.

WHEN some new system in religion is broached, or a popular delusion springs up, they who are carried away by them are those who never knew by experience that word of truth and wisdom, "It is a good thing that the heart be established with grace." We need so to instruct the people in systematic divinity that they will be furnished with defences against cunningly devised fables and winds of doctrine.

THE intrepid conduct of Jonathan and his armor-bearer had a wonderful effect in turning the tide of war in favor of Israel; so that, but for Saul's folly, they would have almost destroyed the Philistines. See what one public-spirited man can do in a church or corporation. People need leaders. If but one man will show himself efficient and competent, a host will often follow, who would not lead.

SEVERITY, and, much more, unfairness, in a judge, mars the effect of justice. No doubt the last judgment will so illustrate the perfect rectitude of God as to leave not the least impression of severity on a good mind. Hence holy beings are represented as saying, "Alleluia," at the Divine sentence. This necessity of so commending himself at the great day to the secret approbation of all the good, is perhaps referred to when it is said of God, "Is God unrighteous that taketh vengeance? God forbid, for how then should God judge the world?"

"BUT though he had done so many miracles, yet they believed not on him." Belief, therefore, does not depend on the amount or force of evidence; nor conviction on clearness and power of statement. See the reason in the passage from which the Evangelist here quotes, Is. vi.

PETER moved that the place of Judas be filled. With what feelings must he have made that motion. But for the infinite grace of his dear Lord, one would also have had occasion to move that Peter's place also be filled. But being forgiven and restored, we cannot but respect Peter for being able and willing to make the motion. Learn something from this, distrustful penitent.

BE not ambitious to be thought very good, a saint. This is one of the many forms of spiritual pride. Try to feel and do right, for its own sake, and to please God.

GOD, who had just punished Israel fearfully, nevertheless would not let Balaam curse them.

SOME are not satisfied with those proofs which are enough for a well-balanced mind. We ought to know when belief is reasonably demanded, in spiritual things, and not be continually seeking for evidence. Two hinges, or at most three, are enough for a door; but some minds, in requiring evidence, are like one who should fill the whole length of the door with hinges.

———◆———

ONE of the first things which a physician says to his patient is, "Let me see your tongue." A spiritual adviser might often do the same.

———◆———

COMMIT to the Blessed Three in One, severally, particular wants, sorrows, requests, which seem related to their several offices and parts in the work of redemption.

"SHALL we be judged twice?" it is frequently asked. "Why should there be two judgment-days?" It is obvious that no man's account can be fully made up till his influence in this world has wholly ceased; and it will not cease till time is no longer. The influence of parents, and preachers, and authors, and good and bad men of every description, will be transmitted to the last day. Moreover, there will be others who will be included in the judgment, for good or ill, of every one.

———◆———

NOTWITHSTANDING God was angry at Israel's demand for a king, yet when it was settled, God would have blessed their first king, had he obeyed him, as he blessed David, the second king. Hence, when we have greatly disapproved of a thing, and it is done, and established, let us learn from our God how to feel and act with regard to it.

APPLYING the rule, "By their fruits ye shall know them," to the Holy Spirit, and contemplating that passage in which "the fruits of the Spirit" are declared, and among which "love, joy, and peace" are the "first fruits," we find in the Holy Spirit an occasion for love and adoration in no respect less than in the Father and the Son.

"PLEAD my cause, O God." What an advocate. Seek him always before applying to another. Who has not continually some cause for God to plead? There are always some on whose will and decision our happiness in a measure depends.

IT is not best for us in religion always to be in raptures. We need absences in our friendship with God to try us.

THE written word is far better than the Mount of Transfiguration. For what did the three disciples do there? They were sore afraid, they fell asleep, and they wist not what they said. One of them, speaking of the scene on the mount, gives the preference to the Bible. "We have a more sure word of prophecy," says he.

A LIMB of a peach-tree broken off in my friend's garden had a hundred and twenty-five peaches on it, nearly ripe. "If a man abide not in me, he is cast forth as a branch, and is withered," — no matter how great his apparent usefulness, or his desirableness to others.

ONE object in our temptations is, to foil and afflict the tempter.

DENOMINATIONAL lines and rules are helpful in our imperfect condition, somewhat like ruled paper. True, theoretically, every one should be able to write straight. Some, who think that to write on ruled paper is not refined, put their own ruled lines underneath their pages. We meet with some who are decidedly opposed to denominational distinctions, yet they are as strongly attached to their own way in religion as those are whom they regard as sectarian. They discard the common ruled sheet, but are sure to put down rules and lines of their own when they write.

———◆———

THERE is never a greater longing for more than this world can give, than in one who is on the very point of receiving the utmost wish of the heart. It is a good time then for a judicious Christian friend to speak of spiritual religion and the favor of God.

SNOW-FLAKES are now skilfully copied, in their geometrical forms of crystallization, in cuttings of delicate paper. The originals are "those marvellous things which we cannot comprehend," mentioned by Elihu among the great things of God. Yet in March you will see in our streets the horses with their heavy loads floundering in ditches of miry snow, every particle of which, however, as it came down from heaven, was a pure crystal, each varying from the rest according to Divine skill. And you will have reflections at the sight which it is needless here to specify.

WE are apt to have a misapprehension of the Saviour's power and willingness to do better for us than we think, corresponding with that of the woman of Samaria, when she said to Him who made all things, "Sir, thou hast nothing to draw with, and the well is deep."

THERE is a difference between "thronging" Christ, and "touching" him with the finger of faith. "The multitude throng thee," said the disciples, "and sayest thou who touched me?" "Somebody touched me," said Jesus. He knew that touch, amid the pressure of the throng. Not one act of faith in him is unnoticed or disregarded.

———◆———

ON meeting with a striking passage of God's word, copy it, and lay it back in your Bible. On opening the book some time after, you will be greatly cheered and comforted on reading that passage in your own handwriting.

———◆———

WHAT in prayer does God probably most regard? "Behold thou requirest truth in the inward part."

SOMETHING in Paul's words on one occasion warrants the belief that, to some of his natural feelings, the work of preaching was not wholly agreeable. "If I do this thing willingly, I have a reward; but if against my will, a dispensation of the Gospel is committed unto me." "For necessity is laid upon me; yea, woe is unto me if I preach not the Gospel." Who would choose, for its own sake, to be, professionally, a reprover, a constant warning, opposing men's wishes, his presence an interruption and restraint, and ghostly associations with him dwelling in the minds of men? And yet for the love of souls, and for Christ's sake, to say nothing of the absolute enjoyments which make the work of the ministry the most enviable employment, every true minister of Christ will say, with Paul, "Neither count I my life dear unto myself, that I may finish my course with joy, and the ministry which I have received of the Lord Jesus, to testify the Gospel of the grace of God."

A MAN comes into a church when the Lord's Supper is administered, and sees among the stated communicants one who has defrauded him. The adversary of souls seldom has a better opportunity to keep any one out of heaven, than in the case of this injured and justly indignant man. It would be a noble triumph of Christian principle, but, alas! hardly to be looked for, if the sight of this dishonest man should excite in the other a desire and purpose to be, in deed and truth, such a follower of Christ as he sees this man is not, but should be. The future condemnation of a hypocrite will not make perdition less tolerable for him who should stumble over this false professor into hell.

"TO me every knee shall bow." What bowing of the knee will be seen at the last day! Now that it will cost us something to bow the knee to Jesus, we do well to improve our opportunity.

HEARING the criticisms which some make on members of the Church, the thought arises, Would that those who have such decided views of the Christian life were themselves members of the Church, to afford us patterns of true Christian excellence! The rules which they lay down, and the exactions which they make with regard to Christians, will be likely to be produced on their trial at the last day. "The servant that knew his Lord's will," must expect plain dealing.

THE way to overcome the fear of dying is to understand and practise upon that word,— "And whether we die, we die unto the Lord." If we think only of ourselves in connection with our death, of course we are liable to encounter the terrors of death alone; but if we desire that we may "die unto the Lord," he will regard our death as connected with his honor and glory.

THAT the Old Testament is not sanguinary in spirit, observe that the decorations of the temple were not any of them images or emblems of war. Many things in the temple were, on the contrary, of a domestic nature. Its main representation, its "altar-piece," was "the cherubims of glory shadowing the mercy-seat."

ONE impression which the whole Bible makes on a thoughtful mind is, that God has had exceeding trouble to make this world love him, and that he has succeeded as yet to a very limited degree.

THE name of God occurs four times in the last two verses of Exodus ii. There is great pathos there.

THOUGH we deserve all we suffer, and more, yet God, who is rich in mercy, gives us sometimes compensatory blessings in sorrows. "He stayeth his rough wind in the day of his east wind." David knew this feature in the gracious dealings of God with us, when he said of Shimei, "It may be that the Lord will look on mine affliction, and that the Lord will requite me good for his cursing this day."

———◆———

IT was one who leaned on Jesus' bosom, who was able to ask, more emphatically than the rest, who was the traitor. Peter beckoned to him for the purpose. The putting of that question is noted by the writer who finished John's Gospel by designating John as him who leaned on the Saviour's breast at supper, "and said, Lord, which is he that betrayeth thee?" The confidence which there is in love controls even our self-distrust. "Perfect love casteth out fear."

IF we need to be qualified in heaven for some special service of great importance, perhaps the preparation will be by some exceeding great blessing, as in this world we are thus qualified by a very great affliction. " Instead of the thorn shall come up the fir-tree, and instead of the brier shall come up the myrtle-tree."

———♦———

WHEN we read, or hear it said, that an advocate " appeared " for a party, we may be reminded of that passage where it is said that Christ has gone into heaven " now to appear in the presence of God for us." Our case there needs great attention, infinite skill and power, and an ever-wakeful interest.

———♦———

THERE is a credulity in unbelief which surpasses that of the superstitious.

THE seal is now put upon all our words and deeds in connection with those who have died. Those words and deeds recurring to the memory, now seem important. We do well to live with surviving friends under the influence which the recollections of particular words and deeds now exert.

———◆———

DISPOSITION in children, and in ourselves when we see our deficiency, is in no way so well cultivated as to see the perfect example of it in Christ, and its illustrations in his conduct, and to keep them before the mind.

———◆———

GOOD parents have a special claim on God to support their authority. So have upright magistrates. So had the Apostles in working miracles.

A YOUNG daughter of a friend, when she was dying, asked her father to forgive certain things which she specified. The father did not remember them, and had nothing, it seemed to him, to forgive. It is, in effect, so with God, when we repent. "As far as the east is from the west, so far hath he removed our transgressions from us."

"AND Jesus sat over against the treasury." With him for a witness, let us order our contributions to his cause aright, remembering the scene which ensued when he took his place on that occasion.

HEARING one complain that he did not know that God had elected him, the question was put to him, "Have you 'elected' God?"

THE manner of Christ's ascension into heaven may be said to have been an instance of Divine simplicity and sublimity combined, which scarcely has a parallel. While in the act of blessing his disciples, he was parted from them, and was carried up, and disappeared behind a cloud. There was no pomp; nothing could have been more simple. How can the followers of this Lord and Master rely on pomp and ceremony to spread his religion, when he, its founder, gave no countenance to such appeals to the senses of men? Had some good men been consulted about the manner of the ascension, we can imagine the result.

———◆———

JESUS furnished the technical ground for his condemnation. The witnesses had not agreed. — " Thou sayest that I am "; or, " I am that [which] thou sayest," i. e. a King. This was that " good confession." — " I lay down my life for the sheep." " No man taketh it from me, but I lay it down of myself."

WOULD we think it possible that God should forgive us before we repent? No, says the theologian, that would violate the whole system of truth. Let us adhere to well-established systems; but there is something above all systems in this appeal of the Most High: " I have blotted out as a thick cloud thy transgressions, and as a cloud thy sins. Return unto me, for I have redeemed thee." Here is the image of one approaching another with a bond cancelled, and appealing by it for the debtor's confidence and love. We do this, sometimes, to subdue a man; why may not God deal thus with a sinner?

———◆———

THISTLES should be mowed in a wet day, else the thistle-down will spread the seeds. The best time to reprove and to correct is, when the feelings are inclined to be penitential. Reproof in times of happiness or gladness is apt to perpetuate the evil.

"HE hoped also that money should have been given him of Paul, that he might loose him; wherefore he sent for him the oftener, and communed with him." Poor, base man! never was money looked for from a more unlikely source, and never does the love of it seem so contemptible as when thus brought in contrast with the noble Apostle, and the infinite riches which he was commissioned to bestow.

A FRIEND had nearly a thousand potted plants in his conservatory which were rooting. He did not seem to be so much interested in them as when he came to some full-grown heath, and lifted it up, and said, "Was there ever such whiteness?" — Strange if God does not love you more when you are old than he did when you were young. How he has watched, and cultivated, and reared you. "And even to your old age I am he, and even to hoar hairs I will carry you."

WHAT a scene that must have been of which it is said, " When he bringeth in the first-begotten into the world he saith, And let all the angels of God worship him." Judging from the effect of being superseded here, it must have been a trial of virtue on the part of angels to see one of an inferior race exalted to the infinite dignity of the incarnation. We were then honored; our nature was promoted; we are joint-heirs with Christ.

WHAT a position does a preacher occupy, — such a congregation attending to him, and receiving that which he is led to give them, and in silence, with no reply nor dispute, and with confidence in him. It should make us love those who thus listen to us. We must be careful not to abuse our power in the Gospel. We must give our best efforts and energies to our sermons, in return for the privilege of preaching.

IF we knew and could feel as much concerning God, and Christ, and heaven, as we sometimes desire, probably it would make us insane. We have seen horticulturists pull down the awnings in their greenhouses. Plants may sometimes have too much sun; and so may we.

LOOKING at one of the most extensive prospects in this or any land, where everything great and beautiful was combined, it was affecting to think, — He that made all this died for me.

TO those whose great effort is to be rich against the time when they are old, the Apostle James may say, "Ye have heaped treasure together for the last days," when you can enjoy it but little, and only for a little while. Were we made for this?

PERHAPS we do not make enough of worship,—public, social, family, private, as offerings to God. He expects them, as he did ancient oblations. They take the place of all those pious acts of acknowledgment and adoration, and they are required now, through our Great High-Priest, as anciently the offerings were made through earthly ministers. "By him, therefore, let us offer the sacrifice of praise to God continually, that is, the fruit of our lips, giving thanks to his name." Each Christian is a priest unto God. "Ye also as lively stones are built up a spiritual house, an holy priesthood, to offer up spiritual sacrifices, acceptable to God through Jesus Christ."

CHRIST never tasted one of the pleasures of sin. Holy angels never did. Souls in heaven never will. Can those pleasures be essential to happiness?

GOD seeks our good opinion of him, wishes to be understood, appreciated, loved. The Old Testament abounds in proofs of this. A collection of passages illustrating Divine grief at ill-treatment from men would show surpassing pathos. As one instance, — in Malachi i., — God comforts himself against the wicked Jews by the prospect of repenting Gentiles. "For from the rising of the sun even unto the going down of the same, my name shall be great among the Gentiles."

———◆———

"BUT while I am coming, another steppeth down before me." He makes us think, though he was not one of them, of those hapless people who are always too late, or who lose an advantage, or meet often with ludicrous accidents. They are, however, "impotent folk," as to energy and practical wisdom. Their reading should be largely in the Book of Proverbs.

ON spending Sabbaths at Cemeteries. Better be in the house of God. You will be nearer your friends in heaven there than at their graves. They are sorry to see you at their sepulchres on the Lord's day. Do you wish for a good example on this point? Even those who entombed the Lord Jesus would not visit his sepulchre on the Sabbath. "They returned and prepared spices, and rested the seventh day, according to the commandment." What an unobjectionable thing, it may be said, to have spent that Sabbath at the Saviour's tomb. But these friends of Jesus were right. They kept the unrepealed commandment.

———◆———

THE temptations which Satan used with Christ in the wilderness were these three: Want, Ambition, and Presumption. These include many of his present forms of assailing men.

THERE is wonderful power in death, upon survivors, to subdue animosities, to make men gentle toward each other, to correct their errors, to moderate their passions, to qualify their judgments, to bring in thoughts and feelings of a refining power. So by the Gospel every curse is used for good.

———◆———

A SOUL pressing onward and upward to heaven through darkness and storms, amidst temptations, with growing faith and zeal, must be an exceedingly interesting object to those who are now within the veil.

———◆———

"I HAVE seen all that Laban doeth unto thee." So that we never need fear, if our cause is just. We may suffer temporary hardship, but the end will be peace.

YOU confidently expect to be converted and saved. How in heaven will you probably wish that you had acted, and when have begun to obey the Gospel, and how will you wish that you had felt toward the Church of Christ and its ordinances, and on what principles had used your property, and what end in life will it seem that you should have had constantly in view?

———◆———

SOME of the ways in which transgressors, when detected, try to escape, are, by Flight, Force, Bribery, Appeal to Compassion, Suicide. None of these will avail sinners at the last. "And they cannot escape."

———◆———

SUPPOSE that you could overhear Christ praying for you in the next room.

HOW shall we feel and act in heaven, meeting angels at every turn, and great and good men? and having the Saviour look in upon us, and the cloud, as it were, descending and resting at the door of our mansion? O to live so here, by faith!

———◆———

"TO whom shall we go?" said one, in reference to leaving Christ. The misery of apostates. To whom can they go? Follow them, trace their dreadful, devious ways in search of peace and happiness, which they have forever left behind them.

———◆———

A FRIEND had it for one of his rules, as helping his devotion, to pause in what he was doing and offer ejaculatory prayer, whenever he heard the clock strike.

GRIEF on the part of "the Holy Spirit of God," rather than anger, at the sins of those who by him are "sealed to the day of redemption," is in beautiful accordance with all the representations which are made of him, from that similitude of him, "as a dove," to that closing word of his in one of the last verses of the Bible, "Come."

IT is kindly said, that while we are kept waiting for God, we should hope; and while we are hoping, it is our duty also to wait. "It is good for a man that he both hope, and quietly wait, for the salvation of God."

WOULD any of us suffer ourselves, like Daniel, to be cast into a den of lions rather than be prevented from praying?

FROM this window in the country I see at least a thousand pines, firs, spruces, larches, standing close together. They were there last year, and the year preceding, and have been there for twenty years or more. Each is undistinguished from the rest, but stands there quietly and patiently. Are we willing, if so it pleases God, to be, not "one of a thousand," but one in a thousand, satisfied to be anything or anywhere, as it shall please God?

> "My soul, be humble in thy low estate,
> Nor seek nor wish to be esteemed or great;
> To take th' impressions of a will divine,
> Be this thy glory, and these riches thine."

WE must not write bitter things against ourselves, nor forebode, nor be expecting evil, but the contrary,— "knowing that ye are thereunto called, that ye should inherit a blessing."

EVEN the Lord Jesus himself, almighty and omniscient, would not "tempt Providence" by exposing himself needlessly to danger; but he practised caution, and was prudent. "After these things Jesus walked in Galilee, for he would not walk in Jewry, because the Jews sought to kill him."

BLESSED are the dead, for this, as much as for anything that can be said of them, — "For he that is dead is freed from sin." O word of bliss to one who here chiefly sought the spiritual interests of a departed child or friend : — " They are without fault before the throne of God."

READ the excuses of those who made Israel to sin.

AFTER being loved as you are here by some, with all the strength and sweetness of human affection, you are going to be loved by One who is almighty and every way as infinite in his love as in his power. We do not yet know what it is to be loved by God, and by the Saviour, and by the Blessed Spirit, and by the Three together.

THE wisdom of not answering our prayers at once. It puts us upon self-examination, repentance, the use of means, makes us wait, and it teaches patience, and has a good effect on our consciences.

PAUL gloried in his "infirmities," more than in his "revelations," — to honor Christ.

CHRIST is the only one whom the grave has yielded to die no more. "The first-begotten of the dead." As such he must be the object of infinite interest with souls, who see in him both the proof of their resurrection and likeness of their future bodies.

———

ADVICE to young converts: — Guard against despondency at the loss of first religious impressions. They are not Christ. He is your righteousness, in joy as well as in sorrow, in hope as well as in fear.

———

UNLESS we have kind feelings toward those whom we are obliged to oppose, our opposition will hurt ourselves, and perhaps more than it hurts them.

"IF there had been a law given which could have given life, then righteousness would have been by the law." This means, "It is utterly impossible for you to be saved by your goodness. In the superstructure of a house, glass, paints, lime-work, and soft wood are indispensable; but they cannot make a good foundation. Our goodness is indispensable; but Jesus Christ is the only foundation.

WHAT is your expectation; what are you living for; what is the present great aim and end with you; what would make you most happy? Ascertain this, and examine it prayerfully. "And now, Lord, what wait I for?"

DO we ever know "a peace" "which passeth all understanding"?

ONE of the most interesting spectacles, perhaps, ever witnessed in heaven, must have been the first interview there between "Saul, who also is called Paul," and Stephen. If we ever indulge the thought as to some of the principal objects of interest to us hereafter in heaven, we may well place this among them, — to behold these two men together. What shall we lose, if we lose heaven, full as it is of such wonders of love and joy!

———♦———

ONE of the chief characteristics of Paul is his urbanity. His address, in most of his Epistles, in his most common manner of speaking to his Christian friends, may almost be likened to the manner of a well-bred man toward a lady. This is the more remarkable, considering the imperfect character and behavior of many to whom he wrote. But this mode of address makes his Epistles suitable for all times. See 2 Cor. vii.

IF but a little of God be so distasteful to a sinner, how will it be when he knows him more? If the duties of religion here repel him, the eternal employments of heaven will be his sorest affliction. There is no heaven in the universe to a sinner. "There is no peace, saith my God, to the wicked."

———◆———

NO prophet ever preached such terrible things as Christ, nor in such terms. But love to man blends so with the Saviour's words, that they do not shock the mind. Learn, that with love to men they will allow you to say anything to them.

———◆———

SHALL death be to each of us "the last enemy"? If not, we shall never see "the last" of our enemies.

HE who would feel his heart melt within him at the infinite kindness of God, let him ponder those words in which God tells Israel, " When thou art in tribulation, and all these things are come upon thee, then the Lord thy God will not forsake thee," &c. We should declare it unsafe and injudicious to tell one whom we are threatening, that, when he has sinned and is in trouble, we will certainly be kind to him. " Who is a God like unto thee, that pardoneth iniquity, and passeth by the transgression of the remnant of his heritage ? "

———◆———

THERE is a moral incapacity, and in effect it is equal to natural deficiency. It is criminal, for this incapacity relates only to spiritual things; in everything else men are not deficient in their apprehensions. But for the time it is equal to natural defects. " Bring forth the blind that have eyes, and the deaf that have ears."

THESE exhibitions of the "Industry of all Nations" may remind us of that word concerning heaven: "And they shall bring the glory and honor of the nations into it." If here a knowledge of foreign parts enlarges our ideas, — recollecting old Homer's eulogium of his hero as one who had "seen many men and knew their mind,"—the endless types of character and the boundless variety of personal qualities and accomplishments in heaven, its natural scenery surpassing all the distinctive features of every grand and beautiful region here, will be to the inhabitants of this world in heaven a transcendent means of enjoyment and progress.

FEW things give greater peace, than to recollect how in times of great sorrow and trial we were patient, prayerful, loving, and faithful. God was a witness to it. "Thou hast known my soul in adversities."

A WRITTEN revelation is an incomparable blessing. Is not the cry of subjects everywhere for a constitution, something written, not the will of a sovereign, nor prescription, but the rights and duties of sovereign and subject in black and white? The Bible is to us like a written constitution; we can take it home, we can consult it when we please, quote from it, appeal to it. God graciously binds himself by it. Of all the modern heresies, none is more contrary to human experience than the rejection of a written Word, and the proposed substitution of human conscience and the moral sentiments as our guide. We hear and read many things designed to ridicule the idea of "a revelation from heaven shut up between the covers of a book." Blessed be God that his will and our duty may be thus conveniently possessed.

"WHOM I shall see for myself, and not another," said Job of his Redeemer. I am to see Christ. No one will interpose between us, in any way, or for any purpose. It will be personal intercourse with Him who has searched me and known me. What influence shall this expectation now exert?

———◆———

"SHARPNESS" may sometimes be for "edification," 2 Cor. xiii. It should be employed, if at all, for that purpose, and never for "destruction."

———◆———

A MOST excellent Christian lady, to whom it was an effort to lead in prayer, once said, "It always puts strength in me when I hear any one decline to pray."

IF we shall have rapturous love to our Redeemer in heaven, is there none in this world? There surely is, for Christ is now all which he will be in heaven, and Christians have the same spiritual affections which they will then possess. We little know what is passing in the heart of that Christian friend who sits at our side in the house of God. If the history of each secret place of prayer could be divulged, we should think sometimes that heaven is not " the land which is very far off."

———◆———

"WHEN Jesus therefore perceived that they would come by force and make him a king, he departed again into a mountain, himself alone." His probable reflections there at the contrast of his own kingdom with that poor principality to which he might have been appointed. Thus when the world solicits us, let us as Christians remember how much better a possession we have than the world can give or take away.

"AND the manna ceased on the morrow after they had eaten of the old corn of the land." Departed Christian friends have ceased to need the ordinances which sustained and cheered them here. At once and forever the productions of the heavenly Canaan became theirs.

A GERMAN princess, Maria Dorothea, (let her name live with her saying,) took leave of a Christian missionary with these words: "Christians never part for the last time. ADIEU."

Index.

Aaron and Moses of one family, 93.
"Abide in me," 168.
Ability, on preaching it, 127.
Abram and the king of Sodom, 86.
"Accepted in the beloved," 17.
Admonish, who may? 149.
Adversary, on having one, 105.
Advice to a king, 82.
" to young converts, 195.
"Afraid of God," 28.
"A God to thee," 99.
Agreement of sects, 147.
Alliances with the bad, 32.
All things made for Christ, 128.
Always do right, 62.
Ambition to be thought good, 164.
"And the prisoners heard them," 60.
"An excellent Christian," 120.
Angels anticipate us, 96.
" not effeminate, 69.
" worshipping Christ, 183.
Apostates, their misery, 90.
Appearances of Christ in the Old Testament, 117.
"Appearing" for us, 177.
Arab race, 146.
Ark, a strange protection, 130.
Ascension of Christ, 180.
Ashtaroth, or the favored sin, 100.

"Asleep on a pillow," 135.
Assurance as evidence, 32.
Atonement for present sins, 132.
Atonement proceeding, 88.
Aurora of 1859, 44.

Bashfulness a snare, 38.
"Beauty and Bands," 102.
Begin early to fear God, 98.
Begin with love, 31.
Behemoth an emblem, 89.
Believing and speaking, 77.
Belshazzar not bid to repent, 129.
Belshazzar's sins, 124.
Bible an anchorage, 14.
" and visions, 201.
" is catholic, 111.
" fearless of cavil, 22.
Billingsgate and Gehenna, 45.
Boaz a picture of happiness, 131.
Bright light in the clouds, 92.

Calmness in divine justice, 63.
Canaan, selection of, 146.
"Chariots of iron," 100.
Cheerfulness after repentance, 122.
Christ a judge of character, 94.
" and strangers, 136.
" an example of prudence, 193.
" before Pilate, 180.
" faithful to his trust, 103.
" in common things, 135.

Christ in danger of a crown, 202.
" in the house, 61.
" in the ship, 59.
" in the stead of Adam, 128.
" more severe than prophets, 198.
" praying for you, 189.
" Redeemer of the Church, 30.
" the first-fruits, 195.
Christ's blood has a cry, 74.
" social pleasures, 143.
Christians and heathens compared, 79.
Church quarrels, 18.
Clinging to Christ, 75.
Coincidences, 145.
Comforter, the world has none, 111.
Compensations, 176.
Confidence in prayer, 106.
Conquering by faith, 134.
Conversion of ecclesiastics, 154.
Conversion, its effect on others, 13.
Copy striking passages, 171.
Cornelius's and Peter's visions, 88.
Count the cost, 108.
Country, our, its dependence, 110.
Covenant with ministers, 115.
Covetous, not recovered, 109.
Covetousness, what is it? 112.
Credulity of unbelief, 177.
Criticisms returning upon us, 174.
Curing evils, 158.

Dagon set up again, 153.
Daniel's advice to a king, 82.
Daniel's discretion, 87.
David inquires in famine, 39.
David's parentage, 72.
David's psalms after his fall, 46.
Day of judgment, comfort from, 89.
Dead, freed from sin, 193.
Declining to pray, 202.
Deity of Christ, a corner-stone, 31.

Deity of Christ, a solvent for doubts, 40.
Despondency, cure for, 27, 139.
Disposition, how formed, 178.
Dreams will be surpassed, 149.

Earth viewed from other worlds, 39.
Ecclesiastes, 156.
Education of conscience, 65.
Election, 179.
Elijah declines his translation, 27.
Elisha and Hazael, 19.
End of a trial, 150.
Ephraim Syrus, 71.
Established with grace, 162.
Every one shall pray, 87.
"Every knee shall bow," 173.
Everything changed at conversion, 137.
Escapes, 145.
Excuses of tempters, 193.

Faith in a translator, 144.
Fallen angels first mentioned, 135.
Father of Redemption, 61.
Fearing God, 28.
Fear in religion, 78.
Fear of death, 174.
"Few," a word of honor, 24.
Field of grain, an emblem, 144.
Fir-trees for thorns, 177.
First duty in affliction, 51.
First-fruits of his creatures, 97
Foiling the tempter, 168.
Food and raiment, 138.
Forbearance, 51.
Foreboding evil, 192.
Forgetfulness of benefits, 85.
Free agents governed, 33.
Fruit of suffering, 48.
Future company of the good, 190.
Future happiness unmixed, 7.
Future punishment, apologizing for, 29.

Gentleness makes great, 161.
Glorified friends, 87.

God, a preacher's chief end, 16.
" a Rock, 101.
" appeals for judgment, 119.
" as final Judge, 163.
" beforehand with us, 181.
" considers wickedness, 112.
" does not need us, 17.
" fails to win some, 175.
" fills vacated hearts, 140.
" in wicked hands, 147.
" is light, 91.
" jealous for his people, 164.
" misses our gifts, 102.
" our example, 84.
" our standard, 126.
" pardons for his own sake, 21.
" past finding out, 96.
" sees others harm us, 188.
" seeks to be loved, 186.
" upholds parents, 178.
" your rereward, 8.
God's earnest promises, 76.
" particular knowledge, 76.
" silence painful, 42.
" sinning people defended, 13.
Godliness requires effort, 35.
God-man, 40.
Going from Christ, 40.
Good influence of deaths, 188.
Good kingdom, 148.
Good men all sinners, 94.
Grandeur of Christ's coming, 43.
Graves an emblem, 24.
Growing Christians, 77
Guileless, 124.

Haman and the horse, 92.
Hapless people, 186.
Have you a heaven? 198.
Have you a last enemy? 198.
Having a heart for anything, 34.
Hard cases, 89.
Hazael, 19.
Heaven better unseen here, 10.
" illustrated, 10.
" walled, 158.
" heirs of, the best heirs, 153.
"He hath borne our griefs," 95.

"He will be our guide," 203.
High-Priest's inquiries, 127.
Hinderances to conversion, 104.
Holy Spirit, his grief, 191.
" " in baptism, 120.
" " judged by his fruits, 167.
" " made the Bible, 106, 158.
" " selects ministers, 103.
" " sins against, heinous, 82.
Holy Spirit's foresight of our wants, 97.
" " future influences, 109.
Home influence on prodigals, 49.
Hopeless deaths, 125.
" mourners, 121.
Hope and wait, 191.
House in ruins, 142.
Human nature joined with Deity, 25.
Human race and angels, sinning, 107.

Identification with Christ, 128.
"I have prayed for thee," 15.
Imitation of good men, 96.
Importuning in prayer, 14.
Imprecations other than David's, 100.
Incapacity of sinners, 199.
In Christ, as safe as he, 97.
"In Christ's stead," 28.
Incidental doctrinal proofs, 121.
Incidental wisdom from Christ, 140.
Incidents make up life, 160.
Infirmities and revelations, 194.
Instincts, incompetency of, 58.
Intolerance a proof of error, 156.
"I pray not for the world," 78.
Iron gates, 99.
Irrecoverable falls, 30.
Israel a lesson for us, 11.

Jealousy for God, 75.
Jehoshaphat, 32.
JEHOVAH's name made known, 21.

INDEX.

Jesus at the "treasury," 179.
Joab's generalship, 116.
Job's "change," 44.
" description of the vile, 47.
" present views of trials, 48.
" scorn, 96.
John mistakes a saint for an angel, 87.
John's question at the Supper, 176.
John's quick eye, 15.
Jonah fleeing from God, 57.
Judas "knew the place," 53.
" repenting, 67.
Judgments under the Gospel, 99.

Key-note of preaching, 155.
Kind feelings in controversy, 195.

Labor for the Church, 83.
Labor to enter that rest, 66.
Lambs and their antitype, 70.
Last charge on Sinai, 111.
Law satisfied with believers, 60.
" sprinkled with blood, 89.
Leaving Egypt in vain, 138.
Leaving this world forever, 150.
Left to be tried, 141.
"Let me see your tongue," 165.
Liberality in false worship, 110.
Life a failure, 64.
Life viewed from heaven, 189.
Like begets like, 73.
Limiting Christ, 170.
Long suffering and doctrine, 35.
Lord's Supper in the retrospect, 159.
Losing a friend, an excuse, 160.
Love and kindness, 26.
Loved by God, 194.
"Love his appearing," 131.
"Love mercy," 59.
Love the living, 178.
Love to God commanded, 159.
Love to the chastened, 73.
Loving and being loved, 154.
Luxurious piety, 62.
Make more of worship, 185.
"Make it a well," 38.
Maker and Saviour, 184.
Manners in piety, 33.

Mark faithful with Peter, 113.
Marvel at unbelief, 108.
Mary's sick brother, 16.
Means regarded in miracles, 161.
"Meddling with God," 23.
Mediatorship ended, 47.
Meetings in perdition, 132.
"Mercy" to ministers, 146.
Ministers as workmen, 80.
" spectators at last, 104.
Miracles wisely withheld, 100.
Misanthropic Christians, 37.
Miscellaneousness of Scripture, 86.
Moderation encouraged, 93.
Modesty of greatness, 19.
Money from Paul, 182.
Morality in religion, 36.
Motherless young children, 155.
Mother of Christ, 95.
Muse and work, 81.

Naomi's advice, 108.
Nations losing the true religion, 50.
New Testament prophecies, 63.
New Year, 151.
Noah's preaching and small ark, 12.
No final escape, 189.
None disappointed at being saved, 112.
Nothing to forgive, 179.
Nothing too hard for God, 136.

Obligation and ability, 127.
Obtaining promises, 9.
Old age serene, 131.
Old Christians, 70, 182.
"Old corn of the land," 204.
"Old man," 85.
Old Testament and the Jew, 20.
On being a warning, 18.
One angel, power of, 151.
One indignity to Christ, 141.
One in a thousand, 192.
Only one safe love, 156.
Opportunities compared, 152.
Opportunities to be saved, 28.
"Other foundation," 196.
"Other men labored," 78.

INDEX.

Others made beacons, 30, 84.
Overhearing prayer, 95.

Painful answers to prayer, 125.
Pardoned, 90.
Pathos, instance of, 175.
Paul, a humbled Pharisee, 76.
" and Stephen, 197.
" forsaken," 117.
" not believed, 120.
" on preaching, 172.
" translated, 101.
Paul's "I lie not," 26.
" social nature, 117.
" urbanity, 197.
Peace and holiness, 98.
Peace of God, 196.
Peaceful recollections, 200.
Penitent thief righteous, 148.
People need leaders, 162.
Perfection, 22, 114.
Perfectness recognized, 117.
Persons and goods, 86.
Peter and Judas repenting, 67.
Peter's motion about Judas, 164.
Pharaoh gives up to death, 159.
Phenomenal Christians, 80.
Picture of the sinner's company, 47.
Pietism, 116.
Pile-driving in the mind, 114.
Places of blessings, 151.
"Plead my cause," 167.
Pleasing God, 25.
Pleasure of God at goodness, 83.
Pleasures of sin, 48, 185.
Prayer an educator, 58.
" in emergencies, 142.
" of Christ in agony, 94.
" and den of lions, 191.
Praying and no response, 154, 194.
Praying to the Three in One, 165.
Preacher's position, 183.
"Prepare a place for you," 43.
Preparing to meet God, 64.
Preserver of men sinned against, 107.
Private sectarianism, 169.
Procrastination, 157.

Proof of God's love, 71.
Prosperity, way to, 107.
Promise to sinners, 199.

Quiet usefulness, 72.

Raptures in religion, 167.
Rainy-day sermons, 37.
Receive more from God, 68.
Reflection on human nature, 63.
Regeneration not development, 19.
Religion friendly to pleasure, 19.
Religion of the head and heart, 41.
Removal of good men, 145.
Repentance defined, 122.
" needs atonement, 147.
Representative guilt, 118.
Requital at being cursed, 93.
Resurrection in the book of Job, 44.
" of the body, 10.
" while we live, 42.
Reverence in love, 149.
Revisiting scenes of goodness, 152.
Rewards a good motive, 23.
" are mercy, 45.
" must follow goodness, 90.

Sabbath and Sinai, 111.
Sabbath-morning thoughts, 59.
Sabbaths anticipated, 42.
" at cemeteries, 187.
" future witnesses, 73.
Sackcloth prohibited, 155.
Salvation most free, 115.
Samson's birth and life 132.
Satan resisted, 134.
Satan's reflections on Job, 70.
Satisfaction with proofs, 165.
Saul and free agency, 67.
Saved from sins here, 143.
Sceptical thoughts, 32.
Scripture helps in trouble, 132.
Secret follower of Christ, 21.
Secret sins, 100.
Seed of evil-doers, 81.

Seeking Christ at his tomb, 8.
Seeming success, 87.
Self-complacent bliss, 36.
Self-respect, 65.
Set apart for God, 122.
"Seven spirits before the throne," 153.
Shame removed, 83.
Sharpness, when proper, 202.
Sight of a crowd, 9.
Signal for prayer, 190.
"Sin not unto death," 72.
Sincerity in praying, 171.
Sincerity in God, 79.
Singing at the Supper, 116.
Sinning after blessings, 50.
" against warnings, 10.
Sins changing to blessings, 88.
"Sleep in Jesus," 12.
"Small ship" for Christ, 64.
Snow-flakes, 170.
Solomon, his choice, 83.
" forgets God, 50.
Spiritual ignorance, 41.
"Stones of the place," 113.
Stumbling-block, 173.
Sublime truths common, 34.
Submission to bitter trial, 118.
Success and goodness, 7.
Suffering well, 15.
Sustaining grace constant, 126.

Temple ornaments peaceful, 175.
Theology must be practical, 46.
The "Three," 119.
Think daily of Christ, 75.
"Thou wilt make all his bed," 11.
"Though thou be little," 68.
Three men at the gate, 130.
Three forms of temptation, 187.

"Thronging" and "touching" Christ, 171.
Time to reprove, 181.
Too much light, 184.
Treasure for the last days, 184.
Truthfulness, 92.
Two judgment days, 166.
Two thirds of God eclipsed, 105.
Two visions of two men, 88.

Unbelief against evidence, 163.
" a heinous sin, 49.
" gently rebuked, 139.
Unexpected perdition, 124.
Unsatisfied desire, 169.
Unseen world near, 113.
Unstudied allusions to Christ, 118.
Unthought-of relief, 139.

Visit, power of a, 29.

Waking in the morning, 7.
Warnings ineffectual, 125.
"Water and blood," 127.
Wearying God with sins, 134.
Weeping, two kinds, 67.
Weighed in the balances, 129.
"What wait I for?" 196.
Whole household perishing, 130.
"Whom having not seen," 202.
"Whom I shall see for myself," 203.
Why do you suffer? 39.
"Wise to do good," 39.
Witnesses of us, 188.
Wonders to be expected, 137.
Worldly hunger, 169.
Written word and visions, 168.

Yielding to circumstances, 166.

Cambridge: Stereotyped and Printed by Welch, Bigelow, & Co.

www.ingramcontent.com/pod-product-compliance
Lightning Source LLC
Chambersburg PA
CBHW020924230426
43666CB00008B/1561